MAX LUCADO

LIFE LESSONS *from*

MARK

A Life-Changing Story

PREPARED BY THE LIVINGSTONE CORPORATION

THOMAS NELSON
Since 1798

Life Lessons from Mark

© 2018 by Max Lucado

All rights reserved. No portion of this book may be reproduced, stored in a retrieval system, or transmitted in any form or by any means—electronic, mechanical, photocopy, recording, scanning, or other—except for brief quotations in critical reviews or articles, without the prior written permission of the publisher.

Published in Nashville, Tennessee, by Thomas Nelson. Thomas Nelson is a registered trademark of HarperCollins Christian Publishing, Inc.

Produced with the assistance of the Livingstone Corporation (www.livingstonecorp.com). Project staff include Jake Barton, Joel Bartlett, Andy Culbertson, Mary Horner Collins, and Will Reaves.

Editor: Neil Wilson

All Scripture quotations, unless otherwise indicated, are taken from *The Holy Bible, New International Version*®, NIV®. Copyright © 1973, 1978, 1984, 2011 by Biblica, Inc.™ Used by permission. All rights reserved worldwide.

Scripture quotations marked NKJV are taken from the New King James Version®. Copyright © 1982 by Thomas Nelson. Used by permission. All rights reserved.

Scripture quotations marked TLB are taken from *The Living Bible*, copyright © 1971. Used by permission of Tyndale House Publishers, Inc., Carol Stream, Illinois 60188. All rights reserved.

Material for the "Inspiration" sections taken from the following books:

The Applause of Heaven. Copyright © 1990, 1996, 1999 by Max Lucado. Thomas Nelson, a registered trademark of HarperCollins Christian Publishing, Inc., Nashville, Tennessee.

The Gift of the Blessing. Copyright © 1993 by Gary Smalley and John Trent. Thomas Nelson, a registered trademark of HarperCollins Christian Publishing, Inc., Nashville, Tennessee.

Great Day Every Day (previously published as *Every Day Deserves a Chance*). Copyright © 2007, 2012 by Max Lucado. Thomas Nelson, a registered trademark of HarperCollins Christian Publishing, Inc., Nashville, Tennessee.

He Still Moves Stones. Copyright © 1993 by Max Lucado. Thomas Nelson, a registered trademark of HarperCollins Christian Publishing, Inc., Nashville, Tennessee.

Next Door Savior. Copyright © 2003 by Max Lucado. Thomas Nelson, a registered trademark of HarperCollins Christian Publishing, Inc., Nashville, Tennessee.

Shaped by God (previously published as *On the Anvil*). Copyright © 2001 by Max Lucado. Tyndale House Publishers, Carol Stream, Illinois.

Six Hours One Friday. Copyright © 2004 by Max Lucado. Thomas Nelson, a registered trademark of HarperCollins Christian Publishing, Inc., Nashville, Tennessee.

Thomas Nelson titles may be purchased in bulk for educational, business, fundraising, or sales promotional use. For information, please e-mail SpecialMarkets@ThomasNelson.com.

ISBN 978-0-310-08632-1

First Printing December 2017 / Printed in the United States of America

CONTENTS

CONTENTS

How to Study the Bible

Introduction to the Gospel of Mark

HOW TO STUDY THE BIBLE

The Bible is a peculiar book. Words crafted in another language. Deeds done in a distant era. Events recorded in a far-off land. Counsel offered to a foreign people. It is a peculiar book.

It's surprising that anyone reads it. It's too old. Some of its writings date back 5,000 years. It's too bizarre. The book speaks of incredible floods, fires, earthquakes, and people with supernatural abilities. It's too radical. The Bible calls for undying devotion to a carpenter who called himself God's Son.

Logic says this book shouldn't survive. Too old, too bizarre, too radical.

The Bible has been banned, burned, scoffed, and ridiculed. Scholars have mocked it as foolish. Kings have branded it as illegal. A thousand times over the grave has been dug and the dirge has begun, but somehow the Bible never stays in the grave. Not only has it survived, but it has also thrived. It is the single most popular book in all of history. It has been the bestselling book in the world for years!

There is no way on earth to explain it. Which perhaps is the only explanation. For the Bible's durability is not found on *earth* but in *heaven*. The millions who have tested its claims and claimed its promises know there is but one answer: the Bible is God's book and God's voice.

As you read it, you would be wise to give some thought to two questions: *What is the purpose of the Bible?* and *How do I study the Bible?* Time spent reflecting on these two issues will enhance your Bible study.

What is the purpose of the Bible?

Let the Bible itself answer that question: *"From infancy you have known the Holy Scriptures, which are able to make you wise for salvation through faith in Christ Jesus"* (2 Timothy 3:15).

The purpose of the Bible? Salvation. God's highest passion is to get his children home. His book, the Bible, describes his plan of salvation. The purpose of the Bible is to proclaim God's plan and passion to save his children.

This is the reason why this book has endured through the centuries. It dares to tackle the toughest questions about life: *Where do I go after I die? Is there a God? What do I do with my fears?* The Bible is the treasure map that leads to God's highest treasure—eternal life.

But how do you study the Bible? Countless copies of Scripture sit unread on bookshelves and nightstands simply because people don't know how to read it. What can you do to make the Bible real in your life?

The clearest answer is found in the words of Jesus: *"Ask and it will be given to you; seek and you will find; knock and the door will be opened to you"* (Matthew 7:7).

The first step in understanding the Bible is asking God to help you. You should read it prayerfully. If anyone understands God's Word, it is because of God and not the reader.

"The Advocate, the Holy Spirit, whom the Father will send in my name, will teach you all things and will remind you of everything I have said to you" (John 14:26).

Before reading the Bible, pray and invite God to speak to you. Don't go to Scripture looking for your idea, but go searching for his.

Not only should you read the Bible prayerfully, but you should also read it carefully. *"Seek and you will find"* is the pledge. The Bible is not a newspaper to be skimmed but rather a mine to be quarried. *"If you look for it as for silver and search for it as for hidden treasure, then you* will understand the fear of the LORD and find the knowledge of God" (Proverbs 2:4–5).

Any worthy find requires effort. The Bible is no exception. To understand the Bible, you don't have to be brilliant, but you must be willing to roll up your sleeves and search.

"*Do your best to present yourself to God as one approved, a worker who does not need to be ashamed and who correctly handles the word of truth*" (2 Timothy 2:15).

Here's a practical point. Study the Bible a bit at a time. Hunger is not satisfied by eating twenty-one meals in one sitting once a week. The body needs a steady diet to remain strong. So does the soul. When God sent food to his people in the wilderness, he didn't provide loaves already made. Instead, he sent them manna in the shape of "*thin flakes like frost on the ground*" (Exodus 16:14).

God gave manna in limited portions.

God sends spiritual food the same way. He opens the heavens with just enough nutrients for today's hunger. He provides "*a rule for this, a rule for that; a little here, a little there*" (Isaiah 28:10).

Don't be discouraged if your reading reaps a small harvest. Some days a lesser portion is all that is needed. What is important is to search every day for that day's message. A steady diet of God's Word over a lifetime builds a healthy soul and mind.

It's much like the little girl who returned from her first day at school feeling a bit dejected. Her mom asked, "Did you learn anything?"

"Apparently not enough," the girl responded. "I have to go back tomorrow, and the next day, and the next . . ."

Such is the case with learning. And such is the case with Bible study. Understanding comes little by little over a lifetime.

There is a third step in understanding the Bible. After the asking and seeking comes the knocking. After you ask and search, "*knock and the door will be opened to you*" (Matthew 7:7).

To knock is to stand at God's door. To make yourself available. To climb the steps, cross the porch, stand at the doorway, and volunteer.

Knocking goes beyond the realm of thinking and into the realm of acting.

To knock is to ask, *What can I do? How can I obey? Where can I go?*

It's one thing to know what to do. It's another to do it. But for those who do it—those who choose to obey—a special reward awaits them.

"Whoever looks intently into the perfect law that gives freedom, and continues in it—not forgetting what they have heard, but doing it—they will be blessed in what they do" (James 1:25).

What a promise. Blessings come to those who do what they read in God's Word! It's the same with medicine. If you only read the label but ignore the pills, it won't help. It's the same with food. If you only read the recipe but never cook, you won't be fed. And it's the same with the Bible. If you only read the words but never obey, you'll never know the joy God has promised.

Ask. Search. Knock. Simple, isn't it? So why don't you give it a try? If you do, you'll see why the Bible is the most remarkable book in history.

INTRODUCTION TO
The Gospel of Mark

The drama of Mark's Gospel peaks in Caesarea Philippi. It's a religious mecca. Every major religion can be found there. Temples dot the landscape. Priests stride the streets.

Jesus and his followers are there. Why? If Jesus preached a sermon in this town, it hasn't been recorded. If he performed a miracle there, we don't know about it. As far as we know, all he did was ask two questions.

The first, *"Who do people say I am?"* (Mark 8:27).

The disciples are quick to respond. They've overheard the chatter. *"Some say John the Baptist; others say Elijah; and still others, one of the prophets"* (verse 28).

Good answers. True answers. But wrong answers.

Jesus then turns and asks them the question. *The* question. *"Who do you say that I am?"* (verse 29).

He doesn't ask, "What do you think about what I've done?" He asks, "Who do you say that I am?"

He doesn't ask, "Who *did* you think I was when the crowds were great and the miracles were many?" He asks, "Who *do* you think I am? Here, against the backdrop of religion. Me, a penniless itinerant surrounded by affluent temples. Who do you say I am?"

He doesn't ask, "Who do your friends think . . . Who do your parents think . . . Who do your peers think?" He poses instead a starkly personal query: "Who do *you* say that I am?"

The disciples aren't as quick to respond. One ducks his eyes. Another shuffles his feet. A third clears his throat. But Peter lifts his head. He lifts his head and looks at the Nazarene and speaks the words heaven has longed to hear. "*You are the Messiah*" (verse 29).

You have been asked some important questions in your life.

Will you marry me?

Would you be interested in a transfer?

What would you think if I told you I was pregnant?

You've been asked some important questions. But the grandest of them is an anthill compared to the Everest found in the eighth chapter of Mark. *Who do you say that I am?*

AUTHOR AND DATE

Mark, also called John Mark. Early church tradition holds he was closely associated with Peter, from whom he obtained his information about Jesus. He is first mentioned in connection with his mother (see Acts 12:12) and later accompanied Paul and Barnabas on their journeys (see 12:25; 13:5). Mark deserted them at Perga (see 13:13), causing a rift between Paul and Barnabas, after which Barnabas took him to Cyprus (see 15:36–39). Mark was restored to full favor with Paul and appears in several epistles (see Colossians 4:10; Philemon 1:24; 2 Timothy 4:11; 1 Peter 5:13). It is believed that Mark wrote his Gospel c. AD 60.

SITUATION

Early church tradition locates the writing of the Gospel in Rome. Persecution and martyrdom in that city had created a dangerous environment for Christians. Mark wrote this Gospel to the Christians to encourage and strengthen their faith. He recorded Christ's baptism, temptation, and the beginning of his ministry with his disciples.

KEY THEMES

- Jesus was a savior and yet a servant.
- Jesus gave his life as a sacrifice for humanity's broken relationship with God.
- Jesus performed miracles through the power of God.
- Jesus taught about the kingdom of God.

KEY VERSE

For even the Son of Man did not come to be served, but to serve, and to give his life as a ransom for many (Mark 10:45).

CONTENTS

LESSON ONE

COMPASSION

Then Jesus, moved with compassion, stretched
out His hand and touched him.
MARK 1:41 NKJV

REFLECTION

Compassion describes one of those longings we find easier to feel than to describe. We can see that compassion relates to sympathy and empathy, but it seems deeper. Showing compassion is not so much about how someone feels toward us but is more about how he or she acts toward us. Think of a time when you were hurting or in need. How did someone show you compassion?

SITUATION

As Jesus preached about the kingdom and healed many diseases, his ministry expanded rapidly. Crowds were growing; demands were great. Once in a while, a quick event unfolded that left a lasting impression, such as when a leper came to Jesus. When this leper approached Jesus, he was breaking all the rules. Lepers were "unclean" and weren't supposed to come near anyone. But Jesus looked beyond that fact.

OBSERVATION

*Read Mark 1:40–45 from the New International
Version or the New King James Version.*

NEW INTERNATIONAL VERSION

⁴⁰ A man with leprosy came to him and begged him on his knees, "If you are willing, you can make me clean."

⁴¹ Jesus was indignant. He reached out his hand and touched the man. "I am willing," he said. "Be clean!" ⁴² Immediately the leprosy left him and he was cleansed.

⁴³ Jesus sent him away at once with a strong warning: ⁴⁴ "See that you don't tell this to anyone. But go, show yourself to the priest and offer the sacrifices that Moses commanded for your cleansing, as a testimony to them." ⁴⁵ Instead he went out and began to talk freely, spreading the news. As a result, Jesus could no longer enter a town openly but stayed outside in lonely places. Yet the people still came to him from everywhere.

New King James Version

⁴⁰ Now a leper came to Him, imploring Him, kneeling down to Him and saying to Him, "If You are willing, You can make me clean." ⁴¹ Then Jesus, moved with compassion, stretched out His hand and touched him, and said to him, "I am willing; be cleansed." ⁴² As soon as He had spoken, immediately the leprosy left him, and he was cleansed.

⁴³ And He strictly warned him and sent him away at once, ⁴⁴ and said to him, "See that you say nothing to anyone; but go your way, show yourself to the priest, and offer for your cleansing those things which Moses commanded, as a testimony to them."

⁴⁵ However, he went out and began to proclaim it freely, and to spread the matter, so that Jesus could no longer openly enter the city, but was outside in deserted places; and they came to Him from every direction.

EXPLORATION

1. What does the leper's statement reveal about his belief in Jesus?

_____

_____

2. Jesus could have healed the leper simply by speaking to him. Why do you think Jesus instead reached out and touched him?

_____

_____

3. Lepers were the outcasts of society and were forced to live outside the city limits. Why did this leper approach Jesus?

_____

_____

_____

4. What did Jesus instruct the man to do after he was healed? Why do you think Jesus commanded him to do this?

_____

_____

_____

5. Why didn't the leper obey Jesus' request to keep quiet?

_____

_____

_____

6. What do you think the leper might have felt after Jesus touched him and healed him?

_____

_____

_____

INSPIRATION

Jesus was a master at communicating love and personal acceptance. He did so when he blessed and held . . . little children. But another time his sensitivity to touch someone was even more graphic. This was when Jesus met a grown man's need for meaningful touch, a man who was barred by law from ever touching anyone again. . . .

To touch a leper was unthinkable. Banishing lepers from society, people would not get within a stone's throw of them. (In fact, they would throw stones at them if they did come close!) . . . With their open sores and dirty bandages, lepers were the last persons anyone would want to touch. Yet the first thing Christ did for this man was touch him.

Even before Jesus spoke to him, he reached out his hand and touched him. Can you imagine what that scene must have looked like? Think how this man must have longed for someone to touch him, not throw stones at him to drive him away. Jesus could have healed him first and then touched him. But recognizing his deepest need, Jesus stretched out his hand even before he spoke words of physical and spiritual healing. (From *The Gift of the Blessing* by Gary Smalley and John Trent.)

REACTION

7. Think of a time you witnessed an act of compassion. How would you describe what you saw?

_____

_____

_____

_____

8. Have you ever withheld compassion from someone in need? If so, what was the reason?

_____

_____

_____

_____

9. Who could be considered the "lepers" in today's society?

_____

_____

_____

_____

10. What would have to change in order for you to better follow Jesus' example and show compassion even to those you find unattractive?

_____

_____

_____

_____

_____

11. What specific person in your life comes to mind to whom you can show compassion?

_____

_____

_____

_____

12. In what ways do you need Jesus' compassionate touch?

_____

_____

_____

_____

LIFE LESSONS

Compassion is one aspect of love. Compassion may grow from feelings, but true compassion represents a practical attention to someone's needs. It doesn't require us to feel; it requires us to act. Sympathy says, "I feel bad that you're hungry." Empathy says, "I know something about how you feel; I was hungry once myself." But compassion says, "Friend, let's go get something to eat." Sympathy and empathy don't require us to do anything, but compassion will cause us to touch, lift, feed, and help those in need as Jesus did for the leper.

DEVOTION

Jesus, you set the bar of compassion high, but you promised to help us meet it. Teach us to practice a different way of seeing people. We look to evaluate, and we look to criticize. We look to feel sorry, and we even look to feel superior to others. But help us instead to look for opportunities to practice compassion. Energize us to move beyond our feelings into the territory of treating people the way you treated them.

JOURNALING

What are some practical ways that you can reach out in compassion to those around you?

FOR FURTHER READING

To complete the Gospel of Mark during this twelve-part study, read Mark 1:1–45. For more Bible passages about Jesus' compassion, read Matthew 8:15; 9:36; 14:14; 15:32; 20:34; Mark 10:13–16; Luke 7:13; 22:51; and John 11:35.

HEALING AND FORGIVENESS

"Which is easier: to say to this paralyzed man, 'Your sins are forgiven,' or to say, 'Get up, take your mat and walk'? But I want you to know that the Son of Man has authority on earth to forgive sins."

MARK 2:9–10

REFLECTION

Most of us know someone who has been healed physically, emotionally, or spiritually. Perhaps that someone is the person we see in the mirror. What were the circumstances surrounding that person's healing? What was more amazing to you: the fact of the healing or the way it came about? Why?

SITUATION

As we saw in the last lesson, Jesus could hardly turn around without meeting people with needs. The audience pressed in and sometimes crowded out those with very real needs. The following event illustrates how far some friends were willing to go to get help for someone they loved. It also demonstrates that Jesus sees past the obvious needs to the deeper ones.

OBSERVATION

Read Mark 2:1–12 from the New International Version or the New King James Version.

NEW INTERNATIONAL VERSION

[1] A few days later, when Jesus again entered Capernaum, the people heard that he had come home. [2] They gathered in such large numbers that there was no room left, not even outside the door, and he preached the word to them. [3] Some men came, bringing to him a paralyzed man, carried by four of them. [4] Since they could not get him to Jesus because

of the crowd, they made an opening in the roof above Jesus by digging through it and then lowered the mat the man was lying on. [5] When Jesus saw their faith, he said to the paralyzed man, "Son, your sins are forgiven."

[6] Now some teachers of the law were sitting there, thinking to themselves, [7] "Why does this fellow talk like that? He's blaspheming! Who can forgive sins but God alone?"

[8] Immediately Jesus knew in his spirit that this was what they were thinking in their hearts, and he said to them, "Why are you thinking these things? [9] Which is easier: to say to this paralyzed man, 'Your sins are forgiven,' or to say, 'Get up, take your mat and walk'? [10] But I want you to know that the Son of Man has authority on earth to forgive sins." So he said to the man, [11] "I tell you, get up, take your mat and go home." [12] He got up, took his mat and walked out in full view of them all. This amazed everyone and they praised God, saying, "We have never seen anything like this!"

NEW KING JAMES VERSION

[1] And again He entered Capernaum after some days, and it was heard that He was in the house. [2] Immediately many gathered together, so that there was no longer room to receive them, not even near the door. And He preached the word to them. [3] Then they came to Him, bringing a paralytic who was carried by four men. [4] And when they could not come near Him because of the crowd, they uncovered the roof where He was. So when they had broken through, they let down the bed on which the paralytic was lying.

[5] When Jesus saw their faith, He said to the paralytic, "Son, your sins are forgiven you."

[6] And some of the scribes were sitting there and reasoning in their hearts, [7] "Why does this Man speak blasphemies like this? Who can forgive sins but God alone?"

[8] But immediately, when Jesus perceived in His spirit that they reasoned thus within themselves, He said to them, "Why do you

reason about these things in your hearts? [9] Which is easier, to say to the paralytic, 'Your sins are forgiven you,' or to say, 'Arise, take up your bed and walk'? [10] But that you may know that the Son of Man has power on earth to forgive sins"—He said to the paralytic, [11] "I say to you, arise, take up your bed, and go to your house." [12] Immediately he arose, took up the bed, and went out in the presence of them all, so that all were amazed and glorified God, saying, "We never saw anything like this!"

EXPLORATION

1. What risks did the men who carried the paralyzed man take in bringing him to Jesus?

2. In what ways did their act demonstrate their faith in Jesus?

3. Why were the scribes upset when Jesus forgave the paralyzed man's sins?

4. Why did Jesus forgive the paralyzed man's sins first before healing his body?

5. How did the people respond to the miracle? How is their response different from the way people respond to God's work today?

_____

_____

_____

6. In the light of this passage, what does it mean to be healed spiritually?

_____

_____

INSPIRATION

Whether [the man] was born paralyzed or became paralyzed—the end result was the same: total dependence on others. . . . When people looked at him, they didn't see the man; they saw a body in need of a miracle. That's not what Jesus saw, but that's what the people saw. And that's certainly what his friends saw. So they did what any of us would do for a friend. They tried to get him some help. . . .

By the time his friends arrived at the place, the house was full. People jammed the doorways. Kids sat in the windows. Others peeked over shoulders. How would this small band of friends ever attract Jesus' attention? They had to make a choice. Do we go in or give up?

What would have happened had the friends given up? What if they had shrugged their shoulders and mumbled something about the crowd being big and dinner getting cold and turned and left? After all, they had done a good deed in coming this far. Who could fault them for turning back? You can only do so much for somebody. But these friends hadn't done enough.

One said that he had an idea. The four huddled over the paralytic and listened to the plan to climb to the top of the house, cut through the roof, and lower their friend down with their sashes.

It was risky—they could fall. It was dangerous—he could fall. It was unorthodox—de-roofing is antisocial. It was intrusive—Jesus was busy. But it was their only chance to see Jesus. So they climbed to the roof.

Faith does these things. Faith does the unexpected. And faith gets God's attention . . .

Jesus was moved by the scene of faith. So he applauds—if not with his hands, at least with his heart. And not only does he applaud, he blesses. And we witness a divine love burst.

The friends want him to heal their friend. But Jesus won't settle for a simple healing of the body—he wants to heal the soul. He leapfrogs the physical and deals with the spiritual. To heal the body is temporal; to heal the soul is eternal . . . All of heaven must pause as another burst of love declares the only words that really matter: "Your sins are forgiven." (From *He Still Moves Stones* by Max Lucado.)

REACTION

7. In what ways can you identify with man who was paralyzed?

_____

_____

_____

8. Think of a time when you experienced Christ's healing touch in your life. How did it affect you?

_____

_____

_____

9. Many people need God's spiritual, emotional, or physical healing. In what ways can you share God's love and forgiveness with them?

_____

_____

_____

10. Jesus' attitude and the Pharisees' attitude varied greatly. What does this story illustrate about attitudes that honor God?

_____

_____

_____

_____

11. The friends of the paralyzed man displayed great determination in their mission. Why do you think they were so determined to get the man to Jesus?

_____

_____

_____

_____

12. When has God exceeded your expectations and provided more than you expected?

_____

_____

_____

_____

LIFE LESSONS

When we look at the results of Christ's life and his mission in the world, we are overwhelmed by the central place that forgiveness takes. Like the paralyzed man, we come to God with many needs, but the deepest is the need for forgiveness—the ugly stains and deformities that sin leaves on our souls need healing most of all. How sad that people go a lifetime without having someone show them the kind of love these friends demonstrated for their friend. We need to experience Christ's forgiveness and then, if necessary, carry our friends to meet him too.

DEVOTION

Lord, how we long to hear your voice say to us, "Your sins are forgiven." We may ask you for other things, but down deep we know that unless you forgive us, nothing else really matters. Thank you for good friends who introduce us to you, sometimes against our will. But thank you always for showing us that you know our needs like no one else. Thank you for your forgiveness.

JOURNALING

In what areas of your life has Christ's power to forgive and heal been most evident?

_____

_____

_____

_____

_____

_____

_____

_____

_____

FOR FURTHER READING

To complete the Gospel of Mark during this twelve-part study, read Mark 2:1–3:35. For more Bible passages about healing and forgiveness, read Matthew 7:7; 15:29–31; Mark 9:20–24; John 9:1–12; Romans 6; and Titus 3:1–7.

RESPONDING TO GOD'S WORD

"Others, like seed sown on good soil, hear the word, accept it, and produce a crop—some thirty, some sixty, some a hundred times what was sown."
MARK 4:20

REFLECTION

You can find them in the middle of busy cities, sometimes shoehorned between towering skyscrapers, sometimes perched in boxes on high balconies and even flourishing on the exposed corners of luxury penthouses. Stately old country homes and suburban cookie-cutter houses have them. And, of course, the rustic, rambling farmhouses of rural back roads always have them. Gardens. They come in all shapes and sizes. Vegetables, fruit, and crops of various kinds usually give away their sower's tastes. There's something unforgettable about tucking tiny seeds into the soil and watching what happens. Have you ever planted seeds and watched them grow? What impresses you most about this growth process?

SITUATION

People flocked to hear Jesus teach and see him heal, but they seemed more interested in his wonders than his words. But when Jesus used a planting story, he had his audience's attention. They were all familiar with the realities of plowing soil and sowing seed. His parables provoked curiosity. They sounded like the parables told by the rabbis in the synagogue, yet Jesus' stories seemed deeper, truer, and harder to understand. Even the disciples found it difficult to grasp his points. When they asked what he meant, Jesus told them.

OBSERVATION

*Read Mark 4:1–20 from the New International
Version or the New King James Version.*

NEW INTERNATIONAL VERSION

[1] Again Jesus began to teach by the lake. The crowd that gathered around him was so large that he got into a boat and sat in it out on the lake, while all the people were along the shore at the water's edge. [2] He taught them many things by parables, and in his teaching said: [3] "Listen! A farmer went out to sow his seed. [4] As he was scattering the seed, some fell along the path, and the birds came and ate it up. [5] Some fell on rocky places, where it did not have much soil. It sprang up quickly, because the soil was shallow. [6] But when the sun came up, the plants were scorched, and they withered because they had no root. [7] Other seed fell among thorns, which grew up and choked the plants, so that they did not bear grain. [8] Still other seed fell on good soil. It came up, grew and produced a crop, some multiplying thirty, some sixty, some a hundred times."

[9] Then Jesus said, "Whoever has ears to hear, let them hear."

[10] When he was alone, the Twelve and the others around him asked him about the parables. [11] He told them, "The secret of the kingdom of God has been given to you. But to those on the outside everything is said in parables [12] so that,

> "'they may be ever seeing but never perceiving,
> and ever hearing but never understanding;
> otherwise they might turn and be forgiven!'"

[13] Then Jesus said to them, "Don't you understand this parable? How then will you understand any parable? [14] The farmer sows the word. [15] Some people are like seed along the path, where the word is sown. As soon as they hear it, Satan comes and takes away the word that was sown in them. [16] Others, like seed sown on rocky places, hear the word and at

once receive it with joy. [17] But since they have no root, they last only a short time. When trouble or persecution comes because of the word, they quickly fall away. [18] Still others, like seed sown among thorns, hear the word; [19] but the worries of this life, the deceitfulness of wealth and the desires for other things come in and choke the word, making it unfruitful. [20] Others, like seed sown on good soil, hear the word, accept it, and produce a crop—some thirty, some sixty, some a hundred times what was sown."

NEW KING JAMES VERSION

[1] And again He began to teach by the sea. And a great multitude was gathered to Him, so that He got into a boat and sat in it on the sea; and the whole multitude was on the land facing the sea. [2] Then He taught them many things by parables, and said to them in His teaching:

[3] "Listen! Behold, a sower went out to sow. [4] And it happened, as he sowed, that some seed fell by the wayside; and the birds of the air came and devoured it. [5] Some fell on stony ground, where it did not have much earth; and immediately it sprang up because it had no depth of earth. [6] But when the sun was up it was scorched, and because it had no root it withered away. [7] And some seed fell among thorns; and the thorns grew up and choked it, and it yielded no crop. [8] But other seed fell on good ground and yielded a crop that sprang up, increased and produced: some thirtyfold, some sixty, and some a hundred."

[9] And He said to them, "He who has ears to hear, let him hear!"

[10] But when He was alone, those around Him with the twelve asked Him about the parable. [11] And He said to them, "To you it has been given to know the mystery of the kingdom of God; but to those who are outside, all things come in parables, [12] so that

'Seeing they may see and not perceive,
And hearing they may hear and not understand;
Lest they should turn,
And their sins be forgiven them.'"

[13] And He said to them, "Do you not understand this parable? How then will you understand all the parables? [14] The sower sows the word. [15] And these are the ones by the wayside where the word is sown. When they hear, Satan comes immediately and takes away the word that was sown in their hearts. [16] These likewise are the ones sown on stony ground who, when they hear the word, immediately receive it with gladness; [17] and they have no root in themselves, and so endure only for a time. Afterward, when tribulation or persecution arises for the word's sake, immediately they stumble. [18] Now these are the ones sown among thorns; they are the ones who hear the word, [19] and the cares of this world, the deceitfulness of riches, and the desires for other things entering in choke the word, and it becomes unfruitful. [20] But these are the ones sown on good ground, those who hear the word, accept it, and bear fruit: some thirtyfold, some sixty, and some a hundred."

EXPLORATION

1. What kind of people does the *hardened soil* represent (see verses 4, 15)? What kind of people does the *rocky soil* represent (see verses 5–6, 16–17)?

_____

_____

_____

2. What kind of people does the *thorny soil* represent (see verses 7, 18–19)? What kind of people does the *good soil* represent (see verses 8, 20)?

_____

_____

_____

3. What do the sower and the seed represent (see verses 3, 14)?

_____

_____

_____

4. How does the story of the seeds parallel our spiritual lives?

_____

_____

_____

5. How will our lives change when we begin to bear fruit?

_____

_____

_____

6. What are some examples of what a fruitful Christian might do?

_____

_____

_____

INSPIRATION

Think about your first encounter with Christ. Robe yourself in that moment. Resurrect the relief. Recall the purity. Summon forth the passion. Can you remember?

I can. 1965. A redheaded ten-year-old with a tornado of freckles sits in a Bible class on a Wednesday night. What I remember of the class are scenes—school desks with initials carved in them. A blackboard. A dozen or so kids, some listening, some not. A teacher wearing a suit coat too tight to button around his robust belly.

He is talking about Jesus. He is explaining the cross. I know I had heard it before, but that night I heard it for sure. "You can't save yourself, you need a Savior." I can't explain why it connected that night as opposed to another, but it did. He simply articulated what I was beginning to understand—I was lost—and he explained what I needed—a Redeemer. From that night on, my heart belonged to Jesus.

Many would argue that a ten-year-old is too young for such a decision. And they may be right. All I know is that I never made a more earnest decision in my life. I didn't know much about God, but what I knew was enough. I knew I wanted to go to heaven. And I knew I couldn't do it alone.

No one had to tell me to be happy. No one had to tell me to tell others. They couldn't keep me quiet. I told all my friends at school. I put a bumper sticker on my bicycle. (From *Six Hours One Friday* by Max Lucado.)

REACTION

7. At different times in our lives our "soil type" may change. Which soil type currently represents your response to God and his Word?

8. What tactics does Satan use to prevent you from hearing and understanding God's Word?

9. What "thorns" may be choking your ability to bear fruit?

10. In what ways are you trying to nourish the spiritual "seed" God has planted in your life?

11. What is your church doing to promote spiritual growth of seekers and believers?

_____

_____

_____

_____

12. What can you do to help the seed take root in others?

_____

_____

_____

_____

_____

LIFE LESSONS

At times it may be helpful to think of your whole life as a certain kind of soil and ask God to show you what kind of changes he desires to make in you. At other times, it may be helpful to think of specific areas of your life as different kinds of soil. You are more like a farm than a field, and God is busy planting in some places, tending in others, and harvesting in other corners of your life. Take a thoughtful tour of your life, considering different areas and asking God to point out ways you can be more responsive and obedient to him.

DEVOTION

Jesus, you are the patient sower in my life. You've used others to place certain seeds, and sometimes I know I haven't appreciated their work as I should have. Help me express gratitude when I sense that you are placing others in my life to serve you on my "farm." Lord, do what you need to do to make my fields productive for you. I'm the farmer and farm, but I belong to you.

JOURNALING

How can you weed out the "thorns" that hinder your spiritual growth? Are there some rocks that need to be dug out? Beaten-down soil that needs to be tilled?

FOR FURTHER READING

To complete the book of Mark during this twelve-part study, read Mark 4:1–34. For more Bible passages about responding to God's Word, read Psalm 119:99, 138; John 20:22–29; Acts 2:38–41; Galatians 5:22; Ephesians 6:17; 1 Peter 2:2.

FAITH THROUGH TRIALS

He said to them, "Why are you so fearful?
How is it that you have no faith?"
MARK 4:40 NKJV

REFLECTION

Storms are unpredictable. At times we see them coming, hiding in dark, rolling clouds that fill the horizon. If they come in the dead of night, we don't see them, but we hear the booming thunder and driven rain. Think back to the worst storm you remember experiencing. Maybe you were in your room listening to it, or out in the woods hiking, or maybe driving through it. Think about the awesome power of nature and your sense of helplessness. What were your feelings throughout the storm?

SITUATION

Jesus and the disciples were crossing the Sea of Galilee. Some of them were fishermen and knew the lake well. They were used to being out on the water, fishing, even throughout the night. They also knew about storms. It's difficult to know who was more scared when the wind and the waves got ugly: the fishermen who knew what was coming, or the landlubbers who had never seen such a storm before. The degree to which you can get "in the boat" with the disciples in this Bible passage will determine the impact it will have on your life.

OBSERVATION

Read Mark 4:35–41 from the New International
Version or the New King James Version.

NEW INTERNATIONAL VERSION

³⁵ That day when evening came, he said to his disciples, "Let us go over to the other side." ³⁶ Leaving the crowd behind, they took him along, just

as he was, in the boat. There were also other boats with him. ³⁷ A furious squall came up, and the waves broke over the boat, so that it was nearly swamped. ³⁸ Jesus was in the stern, sleeping on a cushion. The disciples woke him and said to him, "Teacher, don't you care if we drown?"

³⁹ He got up, rebuked the wind and said to the waves, "Quiet! Be still!" Then the wind died down and it was completely calm.

⁴⁰ He said to his disciples, "Why are you so afraid? Do you still have no faith?"

⁴¹ They were terrified and asked each other, "Who is this? Even the wind and the waves obey him!"

NEW KING JAMES VERSION

³⁵ On the same day, when evening had come, He said to them, "Let us cross over to the other side." ³⁶ Now when they had left the multitude, they took Him along in the boat as He was. And other little boats were also with Him. ³⁷ And a great windstorm arose, and the waves beat into the boat, so that it was already filling. ³⁸ But He was in the stern, asleep on a pillow. And they awoke Him and said to Him, "Teacher, do You not care that we are perishing?"

³⁹ Then He arose and rebuked the wind, and said to the sea, "Peace, be still!" And the wind ceased and there was a great calm. ⁴⁰ But He said to them, "Why are you so fearful? How is it that you have no faith?" ⁴¹ And they feared exceedingly, and said to one another, "Who can this be, that even the wind and the sea obey Him!"

EXPLORATION

1. What were the conditions on the sea that caused the disciples to fear the storm?

2. How did the disciples react to the wind and the waves? How did Jesus react?

3. What does the disciples' question to Jesus reveal about their faith in him?

4. How did Jesus calm the storm? Why do you think he calmed the storm in this way?

5. What were the disciples' attitudes about Jesus after he calmed the storm?

6. Do you have the tendency to remain afraid rather than ask Jesus for help? If so, why?

INSPIRATION

And then there was the storm. The tie-yourself-to-the-mast-and-kiss-your-boat-goodbye storm. Ten-foot waves yanked the disciples first forward and then backward, leaving the boat ankle-deep in water. Matthew's face blanched to the shade of dumplings. Thomas death-gripped the stern. Peter suggested they pray the Lord's Prayer. Better still, that the Lord lead them in the Lord's Prayer. That's when they heard the Lord.

Snoring.

Jesus was asleep. Back against the bow. Head drooped forward. Chin flopping on sternum as the hull bounced on waves. "Jesus!" Peter shouted.

The carpenter woke up, looked up. He wiped the rain from his eyes, puffed both cheeks with a sigh, and stood. He raised first his hand, then his voice, and as fast as you could say "glassy," the water became just that. Jesus smiled and sat, and Peter stared and wondered, "Who is this? Even the wind and the waves obey him!" (Mark 4:41).

We used to look at such scenes in elementary school. To keep us occupied, the teacher would pass out drawings with the question at the bottom "What's wrong with this picture?" Remember them? We'd look closely for something that didn't fit. A farm yard scene with a piano near the water trough. A classroom with a pirate seated on the back row. An astronaut on the moon with a pay phone in the background.

We'd ponder the picture and point to the piano or pirate . . . and say, "This doesn't fit." Something is out of place. Something is absurd. Pianos don't belong in farmyards. Pirates in classrooms. . . . And God doesn't chum with the common folk or snooze in fishing boats.

But according to the Bible he did. "For in Christ there is all of God in a human body" (Colossians 2:9 TLB). Jesus was not a godlike man, nor a manlike God. He was God-man. (From *Next Door Savior* by Max Lucado.)

REACTION

7. In what ways can you identify with the fearful disciples on the sea?

_____

_____

_____

8. What do you think is the purpose of the "life storms" you experience?

_____

_____

_____

9. How have you reacted to one of the "life storms" you've experienced recently?

_____

_____

_____

10. How has God proven himself faithful to you during a difficult time?

_____

_____

_____

11. What does this story teach you about Jesus and the way he works in your life?

_____

_____

_____

12. How could you use this event from Jesus' life to encourage someone who is experiencing a troubling time?

_____

_____

_____

LIFE LESSONS

In the boat with Jesus were seasoned fishermen and inexperienced sea-men. The storm overwhelmed them all. When "life storms" come, what you *know* can only help to a certain point. Experience tells you that you've got to keep bailing. But having a friend with you who has experienced a storm already may offer you some hope of surviving. When life storms come, your best hope lies with *who* is in the boat with you. Is there anyone other than Jesus you would want in your boat during a life storm of any kind?

DEVOTION

Jesus, let me make it official. You always have a space in my lifeboat. In fact, please accept control. Let me live today and every day based on the fact that you're in charge. Teach me to let you steer my boat through any passage in life. And teach me to trust you when my only hope is in the one who can speak to storms and quiet the waves.

JOURNALING

Based on what you've from this lesson, what can you do to face future "life storms" with more confidence and faith in Christ?

_____

_____

_____

_____

_____

_____

_____

_____

FOR FURTHER READING

To complete the book of Mark during this twelve-part study, read Mark 4:35–5:20. For more Bible passages about enduring trials, read Matthew 11:28–30; John 15:18; 16:33; Romans 5:1–5; 8:28; 2 Corinthians 6:3–13; Philippians 3:7–11; James 1:2–4.

STEP OUT IN FAITH

When she heard about Jesus, she came up behind him in the crowd and touched his cloak, because she thought, "If I just touch his clothes, I will be healed."
MARK 5:27–28

REFLECTION

Every day presents opportunities for exercising faith. Sometimes getting out of bed to face the day can feel like a major step of faith. Throughout the day we have decisions to make, challenges to meet, and often we face unexpected hardships or tragedies that require a step of faith. In the passage for this lesson, we see this daily faith principle illustrated in Jesus' life and in the lives of the people who approached him with their requests. Think of a time when you took a step of faith toward God in a difficult situation. What did you do, and how did God respond?

SITUATION

Jesus had ministered for a brief time in the country of the Gadarenes, where he healed a demon-possessed man. Then he moved to the northern end of the Sea of Galilee, where crowds awaited his return. Among them was a desperate father with a very sick daughter. He hoped Jesus might heal her. Hidden in the multitude was also a woman with a terrible secret. She hoped to be healed anonymously. Each of them took a step of faith.

OBSERVATION

Read Mark 5:21–42 from the New International Version or the New King James Version.

NEW INTERNATIONAL VERSION

21 When Jesus had again crossed over by boat to the other side of the lake, a large crowd gathered around him while he was by the lake. 22 Then one of the synagogue leaders, named Jairus, came, and when he saw Jesus, he fell at his feet. 23 He pleaded earnestly with him, "My little daughter is dying. Please come and put your hands on her so that she will be healed and live." 24 So Jesus went with him.

A large crowd followed and pressed around him. ²⁵ And a woman was there who had been subject to bleeding for twelve years. ²⁶ She had suffered a great deal under the care of many doctors and had spent all she had, yet instead of getting better she grew worse. ²⁷ When she heard about Jesus, she came up behind him in the crowd and touched his cloak, ²⁸ because she thought, "If I just touch his clothes, I will be healed." ²⁹ Immediately her bleeding stopped and she felt in her body that she was freed from her suffering.

³⁰ At once Jesus realized that power had gone out from him. He turned around in the crowd and asked, "Who touched my clothes?"

³¹ "You see the people crowding against you," his disciples answered, "and yet you can ask, 'Who touched me?'"

³² But Jesus kept looking around to see who had done it. ³³ Then the woman, knowing what had happened to her, came and fell at his feet and, trembling with fear, told him the whole truth. ³⁴ He said to her, "Daughter, your faith has healed you. Go in peace and be freed from your suffering."

³⁵ While Jesus was still speaking, some people came from the house of Jairus, the synagogue leader. "Your daughter is dead," they said. "Why bother the teacher anymore?"

³⁶ Overhearing what they said, Jesus told him, "Don't be afraid; just believe."

³⁷ He did not let anyone follow him except Peter, James and John the brother of James. ³⁸ When they came to the home of the synagogue leader, Jesus saw a commotion, with people crying and wailing loudly. ³⁹ He went in and said to them, "Why all this commotion and wailing? The child is not dead but asleep." ⁴⁰ But they laughed at him.

After he put them all out, he took the child's father and mother and the disciples who were with him, and went in where the child was. ⁴¹ He took her by the hand and said to her, "Talitha koum!" (which means "Little girl, I say to you, get up!"). ⁴² Immediately the girl stood up and began to walk around (she was twelve years old). At this they were completely astonished.

New King James Version

²¹ Now when Jesus had crossed over again by boat to the other side, a great multitude gathered to Him; and He was by the sea. ²² And behold, one of the rulers of the synagogue came, Jairus by name. And when he saw Him, he fell at His feet ²³ and begged Him earnestly, saying, "My little daughter lies at the point of death. Come and lay Your hands on her, that she may be healed, and she will live." ²⁴ So Jesus went with him, and a great multitude followed Him and thronged Him.

²⁵ Now a certain woman had a flow of blood for twelve years, ²⁶ and had suffered many things from many physicians. She had spent all that she had and was no better, but rather grew worse. ²⁷ When she heard about Jesus, she came behind Him in the crowd and touched His garment. ²⁸ For she said, "If only I may touch His clothes, I shall be made well."

²⁹ Immediately the fountain of her blood was dried up, and she felt in her body that she was healed of the affliction. ³⁰ And Jesus, immediately knowing in Himself that power had gone out of Him, turned around in the crowd and said, "Who touched My clothes?"

³¹ But His disciples said to Him, "You see the multitude thronging You, and You say, 'Who touched Me?'"

³² And He looked around to see her who had done this thing. ³³ But the woman, fearing and trembling, knowing what had happened to her, came and fell down before Him and told Him the whole truth. ³⁴ And He said to her, "Daughter, your faith has made you well. Go in peace, and be healed of your affliction."

³⁵ While He was still speaking, some came from the ruler of the synagogue's house who said, "Your daughter is dead. Why trouble the Teacher any further?"

³⁶ As soon as Jesus heard the word that was spoken, He said to the ruler of the synagogue, "Do not be afraid; only believe." ³⁷ And He permitted no one to follow Him except Peter, James, and John the brother of James. ³⁸ Then He came to the house of the ruler of the synagogue, and saw a tumult and those who wept and wailed loudly. ³⁹ When He came in, He said to them, "Why make this commotion and weep? The child is not dead, but sleeping."

⁴⁰ And they ridiculed Him. But when He had put them all outside, He took the father and the mother of the child, and those who were with Him, and entered where the child was lying. ⁴¹ Then He took the child by the hand, and said to her, "Talitha, cumi," which is translated, "Little girl, I say to you, arise." ⁴² Immediately the girl arose and walked, for she was twelve years of age. And they were overcome with great amazement.

EXPLORATION

1. Why is it surprising that Jairus, given his position in Jewish society, publicly approached Jesus and begged him to heal his daughter?

_____

_____

_____

2. What made it difficult for the woman who was bleeding to approach Jesus?

_____

_____

_____

3. Why was the woman so determined to just get close enough to touch Jesus' cloak?

_____

_____

_____

4. How do you think Jairus felt when Jesus stopped to heal the woman?

_____

_____

_____

5. Why do you suppose Jesus stopped everything he was doing to point out the woman?

_____

_____

_____

_____

6. What does the story of Jairus and the woman reveal about faith?

_____

_____

_____

INSPIRATION

A chronic menstrual disorder. A perpetual issue of blood. Such a condition would be difficult for any woman of any era. But for a Jewess, nothing could be worse. No part of her life was left unaffected.

Sexually . . . she could not touch her husband. Maternally . . . she could not bear children.

Domestically . . . anything she touched was considered unclean. No washing dishes. No sweeping floors.

Spiritually . . . she was not allowed to enter the temple. She was physically exhausted and socially ostracized.

She had sought help "under the care of many doctors." . . .

She was a bruised reed. She awoke daily in a body that no one wanted. She is down to her last prayer. And on the day we encounter her, she's about to pray it.

By the time she gets to Jesus, he is surrounded by people. He's on his way to help the daughter of Jairus, the most important man in the community. What are the odds that he will interrupt an urgent mission with a high official to help the likes of her? Very few. But what are the odds that she will survive if she doesn't take a chance? Fewer still. So she takes a chance.

"If I can just touch his clothes", she thinks, "I will be healed."

Risky decision. To touch him, she will have to touch the people . . . But what choice does she have? She has no money, no clout, no friends, no solutions. She hoped he'd respond, but she didn't know if he would. All she knew was that he was good. That's faith.

Faith is not the belief that God will do what you want. Faith is the belief that God will do what is right. Her part in the healing was very small. All she did was extend her arm through the crowd. "If only I can touch him." . . . Healing begins when we do something. Healing begins when we reach out. Healing starts when we take a step. (From *He Still Moves Stones* by Max Lucado.)

REACTION

7. In what ways can you identify with the story of the woman who was bleeding?

---

8. Think of a time when you found it difficult to step out in faith. Why was it difficult for you?

---

9. In what area of life do you need to experience more of Christ's power?

---

10. What does this story teach you about Jesus' compassion for those in need?

_____

_____

_____

11. Jesus comforted Jairus by saying, "Don't be afraid; just believe" (Mark 5:36). How are these words applicable to your life?

_____

_____

_____

12. Many people touched Jesus as he passed by. Why do you think Jesus' power affected this particular woman and not others?

_____

_____

_____

_____

LIFE LESSONS

Stepping out in faith isn't easy, and the results may not be what we expect. Jairus stepped out in faith to get help for a sick daughter, but at first things got worse . . . she died. Other times, the results for stepping out in faith will turn out better than we hoped. The woman with the bleeding issue was instantly healed, and Jairus's daughter was ultimately raised and healed. Often, there will be mixed results. The woman was publicly recognized (which she dreaded) and then affirmed (which must have transformed her). In what ways are you making it a life-habit to step out in faith?

DEVOTION

Lord, I see that Jairus and this woman had one priceless thing in common: they both came to you in trust. I realize this is one of the basic lessons of faith. If I want to exercise trust in you, I must come to you. I must bring my problems, my needs, and my life to you. I realize I may sometimes feel as unworthy as the woman who was bleeding, but help me to come anyway.

JOURNALING

What steps can you take to strengthen your faith? In what areas of your life can you practice believing?

FOR FURTHER READING

To complete the book of Mark during this twelve-part study, read Mark 5:21–43. For more Bible passages about stepping out in faith, read Genesis 12:2–9; 22:1–19; Joshua 6; Daniel 3; Matthew 7:7; Luke 17:6; Hebrews 11:1, 7–12.

LESSON SIX

TESTING FAITH

They all saw Him and were troubled. But
immediately He talked with them and said to them,
"Be of good cheer! It is I; do not be afraid."
MARK 6:50 NKJV

REFLECTION

Uncomfortable or threatening episodes usually happen when we least expect them. We're sailing along on the placid surface of the familiar, and suddenly a storm breaks out. We're going with the flow, and then the wind picks up and the going gets tough. What experience comes to mind when you think about feeling alone or being in danger? In that situation, how were you aware of God's presence?

_____

_____

_____

_____

SITUATION

After the feeding of the five thousand, Jesus needed some time alone. So he sent the disciples ahead in the boat to their next stop. In Jesus' day, traveling by boat was the fastest way to go. Most journeys had to be over land, but whenever a route could include sailing, the trip was often shorter. That is, unless storm winds began blowing.

OBSERVATION

Read Mark 6:45–51 from the New International Version or the New King James Version.

NEW INTERNATIONAL VERSION

⁴⁵ Immediately Jesus made his disciples get into the boat and go on ahead of him to Bethsaida, while he dismissed the crowd. ⁴⁶ After leaving them, he went up on a mountainside to pray.

⁴⁷ Later that night, the boat was in the middle of the lake, and he was alone on land. ⁴⁸ He saw the disciples straining at the oars, because

the wind was against them. Shortly before dawn he went out to them, walking on the lake. He was about to pass by them, [49] but when they saw him walking on the lake, they thought he was a ghost. They cried out, [50] because they all saw him and were terrified.

Immediately he spoke to them and said, "Take courage! It is I. Don't be afraid." [51] Then he climbed into the boat with them, and the wind died down. They were completely amazed.

New King James Version

[45] Immediately He made His disciples get into the boat and go before Him to the other side, to Bethsaida, while He sent the multitude away. [46] And when He had sent them away, He departed to the mountain to pray. [47] Now when evening came, the boat was in the middle of the sea; and He was alone on the land. [48] Then He saw them straining at rowing, for the wind was against them. Now about the fourth watch of the night He came to them, walking on the sea, and would have passed them by. [49] And when they saw Him walking on the sea, they supposed it was a ghost, and cried out; [50] for they all saw Him and were troubled. But immediately He talked with them and said to them, "Be of good cheer! It is I; do not be afraid." [51] Then He went up into the boat to them, and the wind ceased. And they were greatly amazed in themselves beyond measure, and marveled.

EXPLORATION

1. Why didn't Jesus go with the disciples in the boat?

_____

_____

_____

2. What do you think prevented the disciples from recognizing Jesus?

_____

_____

_____

3. Why do you think Jesus walked by the disciples as they strained against the oars?

_____

_____

4. What might Jesus have been trying to teach the disciples through this experience?

_____

_____

5. What can you learn from the disciples' experience?

_____

_____

6. What are some reasons why God may decide to test our faith?

_____

_____

INSPIRATION

The presence of troubles doesn't surprise us. The absence of God, however, undoes us. We can deal with the ambulance if God is in it. We can stomach the ICU if God is in it. We can face the empty house if God is in it.

Is he?

Matthew would like to answer that question for you. The walls falling around him were made of water. No roof collapsed, but it seemed as though the sky had. A storm on the Sea of Galilee was akin to a sumo wrestler's belly flop on a kiddy pool. The northern valley acted like a wind tunnel, compressing and hosing squalls onto the lake. Waves as tall as ten feet were common.

The account begins at nightfall. Jesus is on the mountain in prayer, and the disciples are in the boat in fear. . . . When does Christ come to them? At three o'clock in the morning! If "evening" began at six o'clock and Christ came at three in the morning, the disciples were alone in the storm for nine hours! Nine tempestuous hours. Long enough for more than one disciple to ask, "Where is Jesus? He knows we are in the boat. For heaven's sake, it was his idea. Is God anywhere near?"

And from within the storm comes an unmistakable voice: "I am."

Wet robe, soaked hair. Waves slapping his waist and rain stinging his face. Jesus speaks to them at once. . . . A literal translation of his announcement results in "Courage! I am! Don't be afraid." Translators tinker with his words for obvious reasons. "I am" sounds truncated. "I am here" or "It is I" feels more complete. But what Jesus shouted in the storm was simply the magisterial: "I am." . . .

From the center of the storm, the unwavering Jesus shouts, "I am." Tall in the Trade Tower wreckage. Bold against the Galilean waves. ICU, battlefield, boardroom, prison cell, or maternity ward—whatever your storm, "I am." (From *Next Door Savior* by Max Lucado.)

REACTION

7. In what ways has your faith been tested recently by the storms in your life?

_____

_____

_____

8. How has Jesus responded to you during your test of faith?

_____

_____

_____

9. Jesus calmed the disciples in their greatest moment of fear by reassuring them of his identity. How does knowing Jesus help during times of testing?

10. What can you do to strengthen your faith for times of testing?

11. How have the victorious experiences of others helped your faith grow?

12. In what ways can your testing be a tool of evangelism for others?

LIFE LESSONS

Unlike the earlier storm that Jesus stilled (see Mark 4:35–41), this one merely stirred up winds and waves that resisted the disciples' progress. The disciples were working hard. Absorbed in their own efforts, they apparently almost missed Jesus walking by on the water. They were probably wondering why he hadn't accompanied them on the trip, yet they were surprised and even fearful when he suddenly appeared. When we get so wrapped up in the challenges of life—or even in obeying Christ's direction—that we lose a sense of his presence, we have shifted our focus to the wrong thing. In such instances, God will often send tests our way to call our attention back to Jesus.

DEVOTION

Lord Jesus, don't ever let me get so wrapped up in serving you that I stop watching for you. Remind me that resistance and hardship sometimes come to help me see that your purposes have less to do with what I accomplish and more to do with what you accomplish in and through me. Help me trust that whatever you need to do to accomplish your purposes in my life, you will do, and at the perfect moment. Teach me to count on you even when I can't see you.

JOURNALING

When testing comes, how can you remind yourself that Jesus is always there, even if you can't "see" him? Explain.

FOR FURTHER READING

To complete the book of Mark during this twelve-part study, read Mark 6:1–56. For more Bible passages about testing faith, read Psalm 112:8; John 16:33; 18:15–18, 25–27; 1 Corinthians 16:13; Hebrews 11:7–12.

GOD'S TRUTH VERSUS TRADITION

[Jesus] continued, "You have a fine way of setting aside the commands of God in order to observe your own traditions!"

MARK 7:9

REFLECTION

Tradition. Habits carved in stone. Familiar patterns of behavior. Traditions almost always have a colorful history, but many who practice traditions faithfully have no idea how and why they started. Traditions often take on the aura of law. What may have been a specific way to express certain core values becomes much less effective if the values have been forgotten. Which of your family traditions would you find difficult to change? Why?

_____

_____

_____

SITUATION

Jesus' popularity sparked envy and concern among the religious leaders of his time. He was breaking too many rules. His disciples were playing fast and loose with tradition. A huge collection of rules for living had gradually developed that were supposed to reflect the central teaching of God's Word. In fact, many of these turned out to be subtle ways to deflect and contradict God's instructions, as Jesus illustrated in the following episode.

OBSERVATION

_Read Mark 7:1–23 from the New International
Version or the New King James Version._

New International Version
[1] The Pharisees and some of the teachers of the law who had come from Jerusalem gathered around Jesus [2] and saw some of his disciples eating food with hands that were defiled, that is, unwashed. [3] (The Pharisees and all the Jews do not eat unless they give their hands a ceremonial

washing, holding to the tradition of the elders. ⁴ When they come from the marketplace they do not eat unless they wash. And they observe many other traditions, such as the washing of cups, pitchers and kettles.)

⁵ So the Pharisees and teachers of the law asked Jesus, "Why don't your disciples live according to the tradition of the elders instead of eating their food with defiled hands?"

⁶ He replied, "Isaiah was right when he prophesied about you hypocrites; as it is written:

"'These people honor me with their lips,
   but their hearts are far from me.
⁷ They worship me in vain;
   their teachings are merely human rules.'

⁸ You have let go of the commands of God and are holding on to human traditions."

⁹ And he continued, "You have a fine way of setting aside the commands of God in order to observe your own traditions! ¹⁰ For Moses said, 'Honor your father and mother,' and, 'Anyone who curses their father or mother is to be put to death.' ¹¹ But you say that if anyone declares that what might have been used to help their father or mother is Corban (that is, devoted to God)—¹² then you no longer let them do anything for their father or mother. ¹³ Thus you nullify the word of God by your tradition that you have handed down. And you do many things like that."

¹⁴ Again Jesus called the crowd to him and said, "Listen to me, everyone, and understand this. ¹⁵ Nothing outside a person can defile them by going into them. Rather, it is what comes out of a person that defiles them." [¹⁶]

¹⁷ After he had left the crowd and entered the house, his disciples asked him about this parable. ¹⁸ "Are you so dull?" he asked. "Don't you see that nothing that enters a person from the outside can defile them? ¹⁹ For it doesn't go into their heart but into their stomach, and then out of the body." (In saying this, Jesus declared all foods clean.)

²⁰ He went on: "What comes out of a person is what defiles them. ²¹ For it is from within, out of a person's heart, that evil thoughts come— sexual immorality, theft, murder, ²² adultery, greed, malice, deceit, lewdness, envy, slander, arrogance and folly. ²³ All these evils come from inside and defile a person."

NEW KING JAMES VERSION

¹ Then the Pharisees and some of the scribes came together to Him, having come from Jerusalem. ² Now when they saw some of His disciples eat bread with defiled, that is, with unwashed hands, they found fault. ³ For the Pharisees and all the Jews do not eat unless they wash their hands in a special way, holding the tradition of the elders. ⁴ When they come from the marketplace, they do not eat unless they wash. And there are many other things which they have received and hold, like the washing of cups, pitchers, copper vessels, and couches.

⁵ Then the Pharisees and scribes asked Him, "Why do Your disciples not walk according to the tradition of the elders, but eat bread with unwashed hands?"

⁶ He answered and said to them, "Well did Isaiah prophesy of you hypocrites, as it is written:

'This people honors Me with their lips,
But their heart is far from Me.
⁷ And in vain they worship Me,
Teaching as doctrines the commandments of men.'

⁸ For laying aside the commandment of God, you hold the tradition of men—the washing of pitchers and cups, and many other such things you do."

⁹ He said to them, "All too well you reject the commandment of God, that you may keep your tradition. ¹⁰ For Moses said, 'Honor your father and your mother'; and, 'He who curses father or mother, let him be put to death.' ¹¹ But you say, 'If a man says to his father or mother, "Whatever

profit you might have received from me is Corban"—' (that is, a gift to God), ¹² then you no longer let him do anything for his father or his mother, ¹³ making the word of God of no effect through your tradition which you have handed down. And many such things you do."

¹⁴ When He had called all the multitude to Himself, He said to them, "Hear Me, everyone, and understand: ¹⁵ There is nothing that enters a man from outside which can defile him; but the things which come out of him, those are the things that defile a man. ¹⁶ If anyone has ears to hear, let him hear!"

¹⁷ When He had entered a house away from the crowd, His disciples asked Him concerning the parable. ¹⁸ So He said to them, "Are you thus without understanding also? Do you not perceive that whatever enters a man from outside cannot defile him, ¹⁹ because it does not enter his heart but his stomach, and is eliminated, thus purifying all foods?" ²⁰ And He said, "What comes out of a man, that defiles a man. ²¹ For from within, out of the heart of men, proceed evil thoughts, adulteries, fornications, murders, ²² thefts, covetousness, wickedness, deceit, lewdness, an evil eye, blasphemy, pride, foolishness. ²³ All these evil things come from within and defile a man."

EXPLORATION

1. According to Jewish tradition, what did the disciples do wrong? How did the Pharisees point out this error to Jesus?

_____

_____

_____

2. What did Jesus find so hypocritical about the Pharisees and their traditions?

_____

_____

_____

3. How did Jesus apply the prophecy in Isaiah to the Pharisees (see verses 6–8)? What point was Jesus making by citing this particular prophecy?

_____

_____

_____

_____

4. What was the meaning of the parable Jesus told (see verses 14–16)?

_____

_____

_____

_____

5. Why didn't the disciples understand the parable?

_____

_____

_____

_____

6. Why do you think it was easier for the Jewish leaders to follow religious rules rather than develop an intimate relationship with God?

_____

_____

_____

INSPIRATION

Once, when we were leaving for a week-long trip, I remembered I hadn't unplugged my ham radio. I ran back in the house, pulled the plug, and dashed out again. But I pulled the wrong plug. I unplugged the freezer. . . . For seven days, then, a freezer full of food sat in a sweltering apartment with the power off.

When we came home . . . guess who got fingered as the one who had unplugged the freezer—and who therefore would be responsible for cleaning it? You got it. So I got to work.

What is the best way to clean out a rotten interior? I got a rag and a bucket of soapy water and began cleaning the outside of the appliance. I was sure the odor would disappear with a good shine. When I was through, the outside of that freezer could have passed a Marine boot-camp inspection. It was sparkling.

But when I opened the door, that freezer was revolting. . . .

No problem, I thought. I knew what to do. *This freezer needs some friends. I'd stink, too, if I had the social life of a machine in a utility room.* So, I threw a party. I invited all the appliances from the neighborhood kitchens. It was hard work, but we filled our apartment with refrigerators, stoves, microwaves, and washing machines. A couple of toasters recognized each other from the appliance store . . . The blenders were the hit, though; they really mixed well.

I was sure the social interaction would cure the inside of my freezer, but I was wrong. I opened it up, and the stink was even worse! Now what?

I had an idea. If a polish job wouldn't do it and social life didn't help, I'd give the freezer some status! I bought a Mercedes sticker and stuck it on the door. I painted a paisley tie down the front. I put a "Save the Whales" bumper sticker on the rear. . . . That freezer was classy. It was stylish. . . . Then I opened the door, expecting to see a clean inside, but what I saw was putrid—a stinky and repulsive interior.

I could think of only one other option. My freezer needed some high-voltage pleasure! . . . I rented some films about foxy appliances. . . . I even tried to get my freezer a date with the Westinghouse next door, but she gave him the cold shoulder. After a few days of supercharged, after-hours entertainment, I opened the door. And I nearly got sick.

I know what you're thinking. The only thing worse than Max's humor is his common sense. Who would concentrate on the outside when the problem is on the inside?

Do you really want to know?

A homemaker battles with depression. What is the solution suggested by some well-meaning friend? Buy a new dress.

A husband is involved in an affair that brings him as much guilt as it does adventure. The solution? Change peer groups. Hang out with people who don't make you feel guilty!

A young professional is plagued with loneliness. His obsession with success has left him with no friends. His boss gives him an idea: Change your style. Get a new haircut. Flash some cash.

Case after case of treating the outside while ignoring the inside—polishing the case while ignoring the interior. And what is the result? . . . Exterior polished; the interior corroding. The outside altered; the inside faltering. One thing is clear: Cosmetic changes are only skin deep.

By now you could write the message of the beatitude. It's a clear one: You change your life by changing your heart. (From *The Applause of Heaven* by Max Lucado.)

REACTION

7. What traditions do you follow that are a part of your religious heritage?

_____

_____

_____

8. What are some things that you tend to do in order to "appear" holy?

_____

_____

_____

9. When are you most likely to uphold outward religious tradition rather than honor God in your heart?

_____

_____

_____

10. What is wrong with measuring spirituality by outward actions?

11. How can you make sure traditions and outward actions do not replace true holiness?

12. What can you do to ensure that you are clean in God's sight?

LIFE LESSONS

We know that external behavior and measurements are both highly inaccurate. Appearances deceive as often as they convey the truth. But that's how we tend to judge other people—until it occurs to us that God is neither impressed nor fooled by appearances. God looks on the heart, and he's the expert at cleaning hearts. Being clean in God's sight doesn't mean we are careless about how we look or act; it means that we take steps to make sure that the internal and external aspects of our lives are consistent.

DEVOTION

Father God, your Son always knew the line between obeying the letter and the spirit of the law. He gave me a good example to follow. Help me to do that. Guide me into an understanding of your desires that keeps the heart-issues in mind and doesn't get sidetracked about appearances. Develop in me the integrity of a clean heart.

JOURNALING

In what ways do you work harder to maintain an outward appearance of holiness to others rather than an inner holiness to God?

FOR FURTHER READING

To complete the book of Mark during this twelve-part study, read Mark 7:1–37. For more Bible passages about having a pure heart, see Psalms 51; 94:8–11; Proverbs 4:23; 2 Corinthians 4:16–18; Hebrews 12:14.

TRUE DISCIPLESHIP

[Jesus] said to them, "Whoever desires to come after Me, let him deny himself, and take up his cross, and follow Me."

MARK 8:34 NKJV

REFLECTION

It's easy to set lofty goals that are forgotten in the heat and drudgery of preparation. Many people are champions in their minds, but far fewer pay the debt of grueling training and loneliness that precede glory. Think of a time when your involvement in an activity required significant discipline or sacrifice. What aspects of your life did this affect? What did you learn about yourself in the process?

SITUATION

Leading up to Jesus' teaching in this passage, Peter had declared to the Lord, "You are the Messiah" (Mark 8:29). This was followed by Jesus' first prediction of his death (see verses 31–33). The contrast upset and confused the disciples. How could Christ die? The Messiah was expected to lead Israel into a new age of freedom and power. But Jesus made it clear their trust had to be focused on him, not on the current popular expectations of the Messiah's mission.

OBSERVATION

*Read Mark 8:34–38 from the New International
Version or the New King James Version.*

NEW INTERNATIONAL VERSION

34 Then he called the crowd to him along with his disciples and said: "Whoever wants to be my disciple must deny themselves and take up their cross and follow me. 35 For whoever wants to save their life will

lose it, but whoever loses their life for me and for the gospel will save it. ³⁶ What good is it for someone to gain the whole world, yet forfeit their soul? ³⁷ Or what can anyone give in exchange for their soul? ³⁸ If anyone is ashamed of me and my words in this adulterous and sinful generation, the Son of Man will be ashamed of them when he comes in his Father's glory with the holy angels."

NEW KING JAMES VERSION

³⁴ When He had called the people to Himself, with His disciples also, He said to them, "Whoever desires to come after Me, let him deny himself, and take up his cross, and follow Me. ³⁵ For whoever desires to save his life will lose it, but whoever loses his life for My sake and the gospel's will save it. ³⁶ For what will it profit a man if he gains the whole world, and loses his own soul? ³⁷ Or what will a man give in exchange for his soul? ³⁸ For whoever is ashamed of Me and My words in this adulterous and sinful generation, of him the Son of Man also will be ashamed when He comes in the glory of His Father with the holy angels."

EXPLORATION

1. According to Jesus, what is the cost of true discipleship? What is required?

_____

_____

_____

2. How do some people react when they learn that being a true follower of Jesus is costly?

_____

_____

_____

_____

3. What is your reaction to the cost of true discipleship?

_____

_____

_____

4. What does it mean to lose your life for Christ's sake?

_____

_____

_____

5. What does it mean to gain the whole world?

_____

_____

_____

6. What does it mean to be "ashamed" of Jesus and his words? What is Jesus calling his followers to do in this passage?

_____

_____

_____

_____

INSPIRATION

The pole of power is greasy. The Roman emperor Charlemagne knew that. An interesting story surrounds the burial of this famous king. Legend has it that he asked to be entombed sitting upright in his throne. He asked that his crown be placed on his head and his scepter in his hand. He requested that the royal cape be draped around his shoulders and an open book be placed in his lap.

That was AD 814. Nearly two hundred years later, Emperor Othello determined to see if the burial request had been carried out. He allegedly sent a team of men to open the tomb and make a report. They found the body just as Charlemagne had requested. Only now, nearly two centuries later, the scene was gruesome.

The crown was tilted, the mantle moth-eaten, the body disfigured. But open on the skeletal thighs was the book Charlemagne had requested—the Bible. One bony finger pointed to Matthew 16:26: "What good will it be for a man if he gains the whole world, yet forfeits his soul?"

You can answer that one. (From *The Applause of Heaven* by Max Lucado.)

REACTION

7. In what ways are you trying to deny yourself and take up your cross?

_____

_____

_____

8. Think of a time when you wanted to hide the fact that you were a Christian. What made you want to keep quiet?

_____

_____

_____

9. How should a Christian's life be different from a non-Christian's life?

_____

_____

10. What do you need to change to be a true disciple of Christ?

_____

_____

_____

11. What is the reward for the person who follows the commands given by Jesus?

_____

_____

_____

_____

12. What is the difference between denying self and self-denial?

_____

_____

_____

_____

LIFE LESSONS

The challenges that Jesus presented in the Gospels still interrupt our lives. _Denying, losing, dying_—these are not the standards the world around us uses for successful living. We're trained to avoid such sacrifices, to look out for ourselves. But Jesus stands before us without apology and asks, "Is there anything you value more highly than me?" We may have a difficult time answering that question, but only an honest answer will do.

DEVOTION

Father, you have given us such a great promise: the promise of salvation. Forgive us when we sometimes put more hope in the things of this earth than in the incredible promises of your heaven. Help us to know today what it means to deny ourselves, take up our crosses, and truly follow wherever you may lead us.

JOURNALING

In what ways are you living for yourself rather than for Christ? What do you plan to do about this situation?

FOR FURTHER READING

To complete the book of Mark during this twelve-part study, read Mark 8:1–38. For more Bible passages about living for God, read Matthew 4:18–21; 5:14–16; Luke 12:13–21; 12:29–33; John 12:25, 26; 13:5–17.

FAITH TO OVERCOME

"'If you can'?" said Jesus. "Everything is possible for one who believes." Immediately the boy's father exclaimed, "I do believe; help me overcome my unbelief!"

MARK 9:23–24

REFLECTION

The little boy stands on the stairs, leaning toward his father's outstretched hands a couple of feet away. He will have to leap in order to be held. He sees and knows his Dad, but the height is scary. He trusts, but now he has to put trust into action. Think of a time when you fully trusted someone to do something. Why did you have faith in that person? What was the outcome of the situation?

SITUATION

Mountaintops are wonderful, but you have to come down. Jesus and his three closest disciples were on the Mount of Transfiguration, where Jesus revealed his glory and briefly interacted with two of the giants of Old Testament days: Moses and Elijah. Peter, James, and John heard God the Father's voice affirm Jesus as his Son. But they had to leave that spiritual high and return to the crowds and face faith-testing complications of life.

OBSERVATION

Read Mark 9:14–29 from the New International Version or the New King James Version.

NEW INTERNATIONAL VERSION

¹⁴ When they came to the other disciples, they saw a large crowd around them and the teachers of the law arguing with them. ¹⁵ As soon as all the people saw Jesus, they were overwhelmed with wonder and ran to greet him.

¹⁶ "What are you arguing with them about?" he asked.

[17] A man in the crowd answered, "Teacher, I brought you my son, who is possessed by a spirit that has robbed him of speech. [18] Whenever it seizes him, it throws him to the ground. He foams at the mouth, gnashes his teeth and becomes rigid. I asked your disciples to drive out the spirit, but they could not."

[19] "You unbelieving generation," Jesus replied, "how long shall I stay with you? How long shall I put up with you? Bring the boy to me."

[20] So they brought him. When the spirit saw Jesus, it immediately threw the boy into a convulsion. He fell to the ground and rolled around, foaming at the mouth.

[21] Jesus asked the boy's father, "How long has he been like this?"

"From childhood," he answered. [22] "It has often thrown him into fire or water to kill him. But if you can do anything, take pity on us and help us."

[23] "'If you can'?" said Jesus. "Everything is possible for one who believes."

[24] Immediately the boy's father exclaimed, "I do believe; help me overcome my unbelief!"

[25] When Jesus saw that a crowd was running to the scene, he rebuked the impure spirit. "You deaf and mute spirit," he said, "I command you, come out of him and never enter him again."

[26] The spirit shrieked, convulsed him violently and came out. The boy looked so much like a corpse that many said, "He's dead." [27] But Jesus took him by the hand and lifted him to his feet, and he stood up.

[28] After Jesus had gone indoors, his disciples asked him privately, "Why couldn't we drive it out?"

[29] He replied, "This kind can come out only by prayer."

New King James Version

[14] And when He came to the disciples, He saw a great multitude around them, and scribes disputing with them. [15] Immediately, when they saw Him, all the people were greatly amazed, and running to Him, greeted Him. [16] And He asked the scribes, "What are you discussing with them?"

¹⁷ Then one of the crowd answered and said, "Teacher, I brought You my son, who has a mute spirit. ¹⁸ And wherever it seizes him, it throws him down; he foams at the mouth, gnashes his teeth, and becomes rigid. So I spoke to Your disciples, that they should cast it out, but they could not."

¹⁹ He answered him and said, "O faithless generation, how long shall I be with you? How long shall I bear with you? Bring him to Me." ²⁰ Then they brought him to Him. And when he saw Him, immediately the spirit convulsed him, and he fell on the ground and wallowed, foaming at the mouth.

²¹ So He asked his father, "How long has this been happening to him?"

And he said, "From childhood. ²² And often he has thrown him both into the fire and into the water to destroy him. But if You can do anything, have compassion on us and help us."

²³ Jesus said to him, "If you can believe, all things are possible to him who believes."

²⁴ Immediately the father of the child cried out and said with tears, "Lord, I believe; help my unbelief!"

²⁵ When Jesus saw that the people came running together, He rebuked the unclean spirit, saying to it: "Deaf and dumb spirit, I command you, come out of him and enter him no more!" ²⁶ Then the spirit cried out, convulsed him greatly, and came out of him. And he became as one dead, so that many said, "He is dead." ²⁷ But Jesus took him by the hand and lifted him up, and he arose.

²⁸ And when He had come into the house, His disciples asked Him privately, "Why could we not cast it out?"

²⁹ So He said to them, "This kind can come out by nothing but prayer and fasting."

EXPLORATION

1. What does this story tell us about Jesus' authority over other spirits?

2. How do you think the father in this story felt after so many years of caring for his son?

3. Why were the disciples unable to heal the boy?

4. What do you think Jesus meant when he said "everything is possible for one who believes"?

5. How did the father react to this statement? How would you describe his faith in Jesus?

6. Which character in this story can you identify with the most?

INSPIRATION

Most of our prayer lives could use a tune-up. Some prayer lives lack consistency. They're either a desert or an oasis. Long, arid, dry spells interrupted by brief plunges into the waters of communion. We go days or weeks without consistent prayer, but then something happens—we hear a sermon, read a book, experience a tragedy—something leads us to pray, so we dive in. We submerge ourselves in prayer and leave refreshed and renewed. But as the journey resumes, our prayers don't.

Others of us need sincerity. Our prayers are a bit hollow, memorized, and rigid. More liturgy than life. And though they are daily, they are dull.

Still others lack, well, honesty. We honestly wonder if prayer makes a difference. Why on earth would God in heaven want to talk to me? If God knows all, who am I to tell him anything? If God controls all, who am I to do anything?

If you struggle with prayer, I've got just the guy for you. Don't worry, he's not a monastic saint. He's not a calloused-kneed apostle. Nor is he a prophet whose middle name is meditation. He's not a too-holy-to-be-you reminder of how far you need to go in prayer. He's just the opposite. A parent with a sick son in need of a miracle. The father's prayer isn't much, but the answer is, and the result reminds us: The power is not in the prayer; it's in the one who hears it.

He prayed out of desperation. His son, his only son, was demon-possessed. Not only was he a deaf mute and an epileptic, he was also possessed by an evil spirit. Ever since the boy was young, the demon had thrown him into fires and water.

What a challenge! He couldn't leave his son alone for a minute. Who knew when the next attack would come? The father had to remain on call, on alert twenty-four hours a day. He was desperate and tired, and his prayer reflects both.

"If you can do anything for him, please have pity on us and help us."

Listen to that prayer. Does it sound courageous? Confident? Strong? Hardly . . .

He said *if.* The Greek is even more emphatic. The tense implies doubt. It's as if the man were saying, "This one's probably out of your league, but if you can . . ."

More meek than might. More timid than towering. More like a crippled lamb coming to a shepherd than a proud lion roaring in the jungle. If his prayer sounds like yours, then don't be discouraged, for that's where prayer begins.

It begins as a yearning. An honest appeal. Ordinary people staring at Mount Everest. No pretense. No boasting. No posturing. Just prayer. Feeble prayer, but prayer nonetheless. (From *He Still Moves Stones* by Max Lucado.)

REACTION

7. What kind of faith does Jesus require of us?

8. When or where has your faith recently been challenged?

9. How have these challenges helped you to deepen your faith in God?

10. How does Jesus' promise that "everything is possible for one who believes" (verse 23) help to strengthen your faith?

11. In what ways does the father's plea, "I do believe; help me overcome my unbelief!" (verse 24) resonate with your prayers?

_____

_____

_____

_____

12. How can you encourage others who are lacking faith?

_____

_____

_____

_____

LIFE LESSONS

The outcome of this miracle in which Jesus healed the boy possessed by an impure spirit indicates why so many of us have difficulty seeing God work. The father's plea expressed a beautiful combination of bold faith and honesty. He acknowledged the need to trust but recognized his weakness. He admitted he needed help and that he also needed help to believe. The disciples were concerned over why they hadn't been able to do what Jesus did. Jesus' answer conveys the point that it's never about what we accomplish but about what God accomplishes in us and through us. The disciples wanted more confidence in their own power, but Jesus told them to focus on tapping into God's power through prayer and fasting.

DEVOTION

Father, we cherish your promises to take care of your children. And yet we often come to you with muddled ideas, uncertain of your will. Thank you, Father, for the assurance that our imperfect prayers cannot hinder your incredible power. Teach us to continually have faith in you so that we truly believe in our hearts that "everything is possible" when we believe in you.

JOURNALING

What are some promises from Scripture that you can memorize to strengthen your faith? How will you memorize them?

FOR FURTHER READING

To complete the book of Mark during this twelve-part study, read Mark 9:1–50. For more Bible passages about trusting God, read Genesis 18:1–14; Matthew 8:5–13; 9:27–31; Luke 11:9–10; 12:22–34.

SALVATION THROUGH FAITH

Then Jesus, looking at him, loved him, and said to him, "One thing you lack: Go your way, sell whatever you have and give to the poor, and you will have treasure in heaven; and come, take up the cross, and follow Me."

MARK 10:21 NKJV

REFLECTION

Dreams of wealth are one thing. Having a huge bank account, vast estates, and impressive treasures are something else. We might be able to imagine having such a windfall, but it's a little harder to imagine what we would actually do with it. If you received an extraordinary amount of wealth, how would you spend it? How do you think it would affect your view of life, people, and eternity?

_____

_____

_____

_____

SITUATION

Three of the Gospels—Matthew, Mark, and Luke—include Jesus' encounter with one particular rich man. He seems to appear out of nowhere, anxious to pose his question to Jesus. He asks a universal question—how do I get into heaven? But it quickly becomes clear that he won't accept the answer Jesus gives him. His wealth has failed to give him eternal confidence, but walking away from the alternative leaves him even more miserable.

OBSERVATION

Read Mark 10:17–31 from the New International Version or the New King James Version.

New International Version

¹⁷ As Jesus started on his way, a man ran up to him and fell on his knees before him. "Good teacher," he asked, "what must I do to inherit eternal life?"

¹⁸ "Why do you call me good?" Jesus answered. "No one is good—except God alone. ¹⁹ You know the commandments: 'You shall not murder,

you shall not commit adultery, you shall not steal, you shall not give false testimony, you shall not defraud, honor your father and mother.'"

²⁰ "Teacher," he declared, "all these I have kept since I was a boy."

²¹ Jesus looked at him and loved him. "One thing you lack," he said. "Go, sell everything you have and give to the poor, and you will have treasure in heaven. Then come, follow me."

²² At this the man's face fell. He went away sad, because he had great wealth.

²³ Jesus looked around and said to his disciples, "How hard it is for the rich to enter the kingdom of God!"

²⁴ The disciples were amazed at his words. But Jesus said again, "Children, how hard it is to enter the kingdom of God! ²⁵ It is easier for a camel to go through the eye of a needle than for someone who is rich to enter the kingdom of God."

²⁶ The disciples were even more amazed, and said to each other, "Who then can be saved?"

²⁷ Jesus looked at them and said, "With man this is impossible, but not with God; all things are possible with God."

²⁸ Then Peter spoke up, "We have left everything to follow you!"

²⁹ "Truly I tell you," Jesus replied, "no one who has left home or brothers or sisters or mother or father or children or fields for me and the gospel ³⁰ will fail to receive a hundred times as much in this present age: homes, brothers, sisters, mothers, children and fields—along with persecutions—and in the age to come eternal life. ³¹ But many who are first will be last, and the last first."

NEW KING JAMES VERSION

¹⁷ Now as He was going out on the road, one came running, knelt before Him, and asked Him, "Good Teacher, what shall I do that I may inherit eternal life?"

¹⁸ So Jesus said to him, "Why do you call Me good? No one is good but One, that is, God. ¹⁹ You know the commandments: 'Do not commit adultery,' 'Do not murder,' 'Do not steal,' 'Do not bear false witness,' 'Do not defraud,' 'Honor your father and your mother.'"

²⁰ And he answered and said to Him, "Teacher, all these things I have kept from my youth."

²¹ Then Jesus, looking at him, loved him, and said to him, "One thing you lack: Go your way, sell whatever you have and give to the poor, and you will have treasure in heaven; and come, take up the cross, and follow Me."

²² But he was sad at this word, and went away sorrowful, for he had great possessions.

²³ Then Jesus looked around and said to His disciples, "How hard it is for those who have riches to enter the kingdom of God!" ²⁴ And the disciples were astonished at His words. But Jesus answered again and said to them, "Children, how hard it is for those who trust in riches to enter the kingdom of God! ²⁵ It is easier for a camel to go through the eye of a needle than for a rich man to enter the kingdom of God."

²⁶ And they were greatly astonished, saying among themselves, "Who then can be saved?"

²⁷ But Jesus looked at them and said, "With men it is impossible, but not with God; for with God all things are possible."

²⁸ Then Peter began to say to Him, "See, we have left all and followed You."

²⁹ So Jesus answered and said, "Assuredly, I say to you, there is no one who has left house or brothers or sisters or father or mother or wife or children or lands, for My sake and the gospel's, ³⁰ who shall not receive a hundredfold now in this time—houses and brothers and sisters and mothers and children and lands, with persecutions—and in the age to come, eternal life. ³¹ But many who are first will be last, and the last first."

EXPLORATION

1. Why did the young man think he would inherit eternal life? On what did he base his beliefs?

_____

_____

_____

2. What did Jesus say the man had to do to receive eternal life? What did Jesus say he lacked?

_____

_____

_____

3. Why couldn't the young man accept Jesus' requirements for eternal life?

_____

_____

_____

4. Why do you think it's difficult for the rich and the self-righteous to enter the kingdom of God?

_____

_____

_____

_____

5. What was Jesus trying to teach his disciples about eternal life?

_____

_____

_____

6. What does Peter's response to Jesus reveal about his attitude toward eternal life?

_____

_____

_____

INSPIRATION

Jesus gets to the point. "If you want to be perfect, then go sell your possessions and give to the poor, and you will have treasure in heaven."

The statement leaves the young man distraught and the disciples bewildered.

Their question could be ours: "Who then can be saved?" Jesus' answer shellshocks the listeners, "With man this is impossible . . ."

Impossible.

He doesn't say improbable. He doesn't say unlikely. He doesn't even say it will be tough. He says it is "impossible." . . .

Does that strike you as cold? All your life you've been rewarded according to your performance. You get grades according to your study. You get commendations according to your success. You get money in response to your work.

That's why the rich young ruler thought heaven was just a payment away. It only made sense. You work hard, you pay your dues, and "zap"—your account is credited as paid in full. Jesus says, "No way." What you want costs far more than what you can pay. You don't need a system; you need a Savior. You don't need a resume; you need a Redeemer. For "what is impossible with men is possible with God." . . .

You see, it wasn't the money that hindered the rich man; it was the self-sufficiency. It wasn't the possessions; it was the pomp. It wasn't the big bucks; it was the big head . . .

Astounding. These people are standing before the throne of God and bragging about themselves. The great trumpet has sounded, and they are still tooting their own horns. Rather than sing his praises, they sing their own. Rather than worship God, they read their resumes. When they should be speechless, they speak. In the very aura of the King they boast of self. What is worse—their arrogance or their blindness?

God does not save us because of what we've done . . . and only a great God does for his children what they can't do for themselves.

That is the message of Paul: "For what the law was powerless to do . . .

God did." And that is the message of the first beatitude. "Blessed are the poor in spirit . . ." The jewel of joy is given to the impoverished spirits, not the affluent. God's delight is received upon surrender, not awarded upon conquest. (From *The Applause of Heaven* by Max Lucado.)

REACTION

7. In what ways are you measuring obedience to God by your internal attitudes rather than your external actions?

_____

_____

_____

_____

8. Why is it easy to fool ourselves into believing we somehow "deserve" God's mercy and salvation? What does this story tell us about what we must put first in our lives?

_____

_____

_____

_____

9. What does it mean that the "first will be last, and the last first" (verse 31)?

_____

_____

_____

_____

10. What should be the attitude of believers toward wealth?

_____

_____

_____

_____

11. What is Jesus' promise to those who give up the treasures of this world for his sake?

_____

_____

_____

_____

12. What, in addition to money, can distract people who want to follow God?

_____

_____

_____

_____

LIFE LESSONS

Like a skilled surgeon's knife, Jesus' words could have separated that man's heart from his riches. The operation would have been painful, but eternally effective. Jesus had already said, "For where your treasure is, there your heart will be also" (Matthew 6:21). His words exposed the man's inner struggle and challenge. When we're looking for what's really in our hearts, the best place to start is with our finances and "stuff." If we recognize that they belong to God and that we are only stewards, then it's likely that our hearts will be in God's hands as well.

DEVOTION

Father, reveal to us today what it is that we lack in our devotion to you. Help us to see the idols we have set up in our lives that we are serving instead of you. Keep us from being so blinded by the possessions of this world, which we cannot keep, that we fail to see the eternal treasure in you, which we can never lose. Help us to put you first in all that we do and say.

JOURNALING

How can you avoid the trap of putting your confidence in things rather than in God?

FOR FURTHER READING

To complete the book of Mark during this twelve-part study, read Mark 10:1–52. For more Bible passages about the deceitfulness of riches, read Proverbs 28:11, 20; Matthew 15:21–28; Mark 8:36–37; Luke 12:15–21; 16:19–31.

THE GREATEST COMMANDMENT

"Love the Lord your God with all your heart and with all your soul and with all your mind and with all your strength."

MARK 12:30

REFLECTION

The central rule of living has to do with love. When Jesus was asked, "What's the main thing of life?" he didn't hesitate to answer. Just as we need to think broadly about ways to express our love to others, we must be constantly widening the scope of our love for God. Think of someone you love. In how many different ways do you show that person your love?

SITUATION

Conflicts and enmity in Jesus' ministry were coming to a head. His opponents, the Jewish religious leaders, were threatened and were reaching the end of their patience. Jesus responded countless times to their trick questions and verbal traps. He showed that he was more than equal to the task. So much so that one teacher of the law decided to ask Jesus a question that had been on his mind for a long time. The Lord's answer left him with much to think about.

OBSERVATION

Read Mark 12:28–34 from the New International Version or the New King James Version.

NEW INTERNATIONAL VERSION

²⁸ One of the teachers of the law came and heard them debating. Noticing that Jesus had given them a good answer, he asked him, "Of all the commandments, which is the most important?"

[29] "The most important one," answered Jesus, "is this: 'Hear, O Israel: The Lord our God, the Lord is one. [30] Love the Lord your God with all your heart and with all your soul and with all your mind and with all your strength.' [31] The second is this: 'Love your neighbor as yourself.' There is no commandment greater than these."

[32] "Well said, teacher," the man replied. "You are right in saying that God is one and there is no other but him. [33] To love him with all your heart, with all your understanding and with all your strength, and to love your neighbor as yourself is more important than all burnt offerings and sacrifices."

[34] When Jesus saw that he had answered wisely, he said to him, "You are not far from the kingdom of God." And from then on no one dared ask him any more questions.

New King James Version

[28] Then one of the scribes came, and having heard them reasoning together, perceiving that He had answered them well, asked Him, "Which is the first commandment of all?"

[29] Jesus answered him, "The first of all the commandments is: 'Hear, O Israel, the Lord our God, the Lord is one. [30] And you shall love the Lord your God with all your heart, with all your soul, with all your mind, and with all your strength.' This is the first commandment. [31] And the second, like it, is this: 'You shall love your neighbor as yourself.' There is no other commandment greater than these."

[32] So the scribe said to Him, "Well said, Teacher. You have spoken the truth, for there is one God, and there is no other but He. [33] And to love Him with all the heart, with all the understanding, with all the soul, and with all the strength, and to love one's neighbor as oneself, is more than all the whole burnt offerings and sacrifices."

[34] Now when Jesus saw that he answered wisely, He said to him, "You are not far from the kingdom of God."

But after that no one dared question Him.

EXPLORATION

1. What did Jesus say was the greatest commandment? The next greatest?

2. What kind of love are we commanded to have for God?

3. What does it mean to love God with all your heart, your soul, your mind, and your strength?

4. How do you love yourself? How do you love your neighbor as yourself?

5. Think of a time when you witnessed a loving deed. What impressed you most about the situation?

6. What did Jesus say is the most important thing in life?

INSPIRATION

(*Scene—Sunday morning church assembly; silent prayer*)

Max: God, I want to do great things.

God: You do?

Max: You bet! I want to teach millions! I want to fill the Rose Bowl! I want all of the world to know your saving power! I dream of the day—

God: That's great, Max. In fact, I can use you today after church.

Max: Super! How about some radio and TV work or . . . an engagement to speak to Congress?

God: Well, that's not exactly what I had in mind. See that fellow sitting next to you?

Max: Yes.

God: He needs a ride home.

Max (quietly): What?

God: He needs a ride home. And while you're at it, one of the older ladies sitting near you is worried about getting a refrigerator moved. Why don't you drop by this afternoon and—

Max (pleading): But, God, what about the world?

God (smiling): Think about it. (From *Shaped by God* by Max Lucado.)

REACTION

7. In which aspect—your heart, soul, or mind—do you find it most difficult to love God? Why?

_____

_____

_____

8. Why is it challenging to love God as he commands?

_____

_____

_____

9. Why it is often a struggle to love your neighbor as yourself?

10. How are the two components of the Great Commandment interrelated?

11. What does it mean when a person is not far from the kingdom of God?

12. In what ways is the command to love God different from the human emotion of love?

LIFE LESSONS

The Great Commandment, with its two components—love for God and love for neighbor—lies at the center of our response to all that Christ has done for us. Our response must not focus on what will make us feel significant, effective, or indispensable. Rather, we must keep coming back to obedience. As we recognize all that God has done for us, we need to ask ourselves what we can do for our neighbor in grateful response to God's mercy on us.

DEVOTION

God, give us strength as we try to be more like Jesus in our lives. We ask you to keep the evil one away from us and to keep us close to you, Father. Let our lives be testimonies of your love for us, so that when people see our lives, they would see how you have loved the world.

JOURNALING

How can you show others a more sacrificial love? What would be a good place to start?

FOR FURTHER READING

To complete the book of Mark during this twelve-part study, read Mark 11:1–13:37. For more Bible passages about loving God and others, read Matthew 5:43–44; John 13:34; Romans 12:9; 1 Corinthians 13:4–8; Ephesians 5:2; 1 John 4:7–12, 19–21; 5:1–3; 2 John 5.

LESSON TWELVE

ADORATION

*"She poured perfume on my body beforehand to
prepare for my burial. Truly I tell you, wherever the
gospel is preached throughout the world, what she
has done will also be told, in memory of her."*

MARK 14:8–9

REFLECTION

Think of a meaningful gift you have given to someone. Think about what made that gift meaningful. Sometimes the gift's significance comes from what you wanted to express. Sometimes it comes from how you think the person would be affected or helped by the gift. How did that person respond to your gift? In what ways has that experience shaped the way you think about gift giving?

SITUATION

By this point in Jesus' ministry, tensions were at a high level. His triumphant entry into Jerusalem had occurred days before, and the religious leaders were desperate to solve the "Jesus problem." But in the midst of the attacks and constant scrutiny, Jesus took time to accept a loving gift. Note that while Mark does not identify the woman in this story, John tells us that she was Mary of Bethany, the sister of Martha and Lazarus (see John 12:1–8).

OBSERVATION

Read Mark 14:3–9 from the New International Version or the New King James Version.

NEW INTERNATIONAL VERSION

³ While he was in Bethany, reclining at the table in the home of Simon the Leper, a woman came with an alabaster jar of very expensive perfume, made of pure nard. She broke the jar and poured the perfume on his head.

⁴ Some of those present were saying indignantly to one another, "Why this waste of perfume? ⁵ It could have been sold for more than a year's wages and the money given to the poor." And they rebuked her harshly.

⁶ "Leave her alone," said Jesus. "Why are you bothering her? She has done a beautiful thing to me. ⁷ The poor you will always have with you, and you can help them any time you want. But you will not always have me. ⁸ She did what she could. She poured perfume on my body beforehand to prepare for my burial. ⁹ Truly I tell you, wherever the gospel is preached throughout the world, what she has done will also be told, in memory of her."

New King James Version

³ And being in Bethany at the house of Simon the leper, as He sat at the table, a woman came having an alabaster flask of very costly oil of spikenard. Then she broke the flask and poured it on His head. ⁴ But there were some who were indignant among themselves, and said, "Why was this fragrant oil wasted? ⁵ For it might have been sold for more than three hundred denarii and given to the poor." And they criticized her sharply.

⁶ But Jesus said, "Let her alone. Why do you trouble her? She has done a good work for Me. ⁷ For you have the poor with you always, and whenever you wish you may do them good; but Me you do not have always. ⁸ She has done what she could. She has come beforehand to anoint My body for burial. ⁹ Assuredly, I say to you, wherever this gospel is preached in the whole world, what this woman has done will also be told as a memorial to her."

EXPLORATION

1. Why did some of the guests criticize the woman for her actions?

2. How did Jesus respond to these criticisms of the woman?

3. How might the woman have felt after Jesus affirmed her actions?

4. Why did the woman choose to anoint Jesus at this time?

5. What did Jesus say was the significance of the woman's actions?

6. Picture yourself in the room with Jesus, the disciples, and the woman. How would you have responded to this very expensive gift?

INSPIRATION

Imagine yourself as a twelve-year-old facing a sink of dirty dishes. You don't want to wash them. You'd rather play with your friends or watch television. But your mom has made it clear: *clean the dishes.*

You groan, moan, and wonder how you might place yourself for adoption. Then, from who knows where, a wacky idea strikes you. What if you surprise your mom by cleaning, not just the dishes, but the entire kitchen? You begin to smile. "I'll sweep the floor and wipe down the cabinets. Maybe reorganize the refrigerator!" And from some unknown source comes a shot of energy, a surge of productivity. A dull task becomes an adventure. Why? Liberation! You've passed from slave to volunteer.

This is the joy of the second mile.

Have you found it? Your day moves with the speed of an ice floe and the excitement of a quilting tournament. You do what is required—math problems and one chapter in literature—but no more. You are reliable, dependable, and quite likely bored. You dream of Fridays, holidays, a different family or a different job, when maybe all you need is a different attitude. Give your day a chance.

Daily do a deed for which you cannot be repaid.

In the final days of Jesus' life, he shared a meal with his friends Lazarus, Martha, and Mary. Within the week he would feel the sting of the Roman whip, the point of the thorny crown, and the iron of the executioner's nail. But on this evening, he felt the love of three friends.

For Mary, however, giving the dinner was not enough. "Mary took about a pint of pure nard, an expensive perfume; she poured it on Jesus' feet and wiped his feet with her hair. And the house was filled with the fragrance of the perfume" (John 12:3).

One-milers among the group, like Judas, criticized the deed as wasteful. Not Jesus. He received the gesture as an extravagant demonstration of love, a friend surrendering her most treasured gift. As Jesus hung on the cross, we wonder, *Did he detect the fragrance on his skin?*

Follow Mary's example.

There is an elderly man in your community who just lost his wife. An hour of your time would mean the world to him. Some kids in your city have no dad. No father takes them to movies or baseball games. Maybe you can. They can't pay you back. They can't even afford the popcorn or sodas. But they'll smile like a cantaloupe slice at your kindness.

Or how about this one? Down the hall from your bedroom is a person who shares your last name. Shock that person with kindness. Something outlandish. Your homework done with no complaints. Coffee served before he awakens. A love letter written to her for no special reason. Alabaster poured, just because.

Want to snatch a day from the manacles of boredom? Do overgenerous deeds, acts beyond reimbursement. Kindness without compensation. Do a deed for which you cannot be repaid. (From *Great Day Every Day* by Max Lucado.)

REACTION

7. Have you ever been criticized for loving God like Mary was? If so, in what ways?

8. Based on Mark 14:3–9, how should you respond to those who criticize your love for God?

9. What are you willing to sacrifice to worship God?

10. In what ways does Mary's example challenge your view of worship?

11. Why was it difficult for the others to see the value in what Mary did for Jesus?

_____

_____

_____

_____

12. Why do you think Mary chose to offer this particular gift to Jesus?

_____

_____

_____

LIFE LESSONS

In this passage, there was a crowd of people all sharing a room with Jesus. They were in his presence. Yet out of that crowded room, only one person expressed her adoration and love. The process of gratitude and worship requires some kind of personal connection on our part. It may be easier for us to go through prescribed motions and follow someone else's cues, but if that is the limit of our participation in worship, we will be left with little in the way of personal transformation. Being in Christ's presence and expressing our gratitude ought to change us. One of the best questions we can ask as we prepare for worship is, "How will I express what Jesus means to me today while I am with others?"

DEVOTION

Father, help us to take time to adore and worship you. Help us to maintain our promise of faithfulness to you, even in times when we are surrounded by people who oppose your kingdom. Give us great courage as we face the challenges of following you.

JOURNALING

How does this story inspire you to pour out you heart in worship? When and how will you carry out that desire?

_____

_____

_____

_____

_____

_____

_____

_____

_____

_____

_____

_____

FOR FURTHER READING

To complete the book of Mark during this twelve-part study, read Mark 14:1–16:20. For more Bible passages about adoring God, read Exodus 3:1–6; 34:14; Psalm 29:12; Luke 10:38–42; Hebrews 12:28; James 4:8.

LEADER'S GUIDE FOR SMALL GROUPS

Thank you for your willingness to lead a group through *Life Lessons from Mark*. The rewards of being a leader are different from those of participating, and we hope you find your own walk with Jesus deepened by this experience. During the twelve lessons in this study, you will guide your group through selected passages in Mark and explore the key themes of the Gospel. There are several elements in this leader's guide that will help you as you structure your study and reflection time, so be sure to follow along and take advantage of each one.

BEFORE YOU BEGIN

Before your first meeting, make sure the group members have their own copy of the *Life Lessons from Mark* study guide so they can follow along and have their answers written out ahead of time. Alternately, you can hand out the guides at your first meeting and give the group some time to look over the material and ask any preliminary questions. Be sure to send a sheet around the room during that first meeting and have the members write down their name, phone number, and email address so you can keep in touch with them during the week.

There are several ways to structure the duration of the study. You can choose to cover each lesson individually for a total of twelve weeks of discussion, or you can combine two lessons together per week for a total of six weeks of discussion. You can also choose to have the group members read just the selected passages of Scripture given in each lesson, or they can cover the entire book of Mark by reading the material listed in the "For Further Reading" section at the end of each lesson. The following table illustrates these options:

Twelve-Week Format

Week	Lessons Covered	Simplified Reading	Expanded Reading
1	Compassion	Mark 1:40–45	Mark 1:1–45
2	Healing and Forgiveness	Mark 2:1–12	Mark 2:1–3:35
3	Responding to God's Word	Mark 4:1–20	Mark 4:1–34
4	Faith Through Trials	Mark 4:35–41	Mark 4:35–5:20
5	Step Out in Faith	Mark 5:21–42	Mark 5:21–43
6	Testing Faith	Mark 6:45–51	Mark 6:1–56
7	God's Truth Versus Tradition	Mark 7:1–23	Mark 7:1–37
8	True Discipleship	Mark 8:34–38	Mark 8:1–38
9	Faith to Overcome	Mark 9:14–29	Mark 9:1–50
10	Salvation Through Faith	Mark 10:17–31	Mark 10:1–52
11	The Greatest Commandment	Mark 12:28–34	Mark 11:1–13:37
12	Adoration	Mark 14:3–9	Mark 14:1–16:20

Six-Week Format

Week	Lessons Covered	Simplified Reading	Expanded Reading
1	Compassion / Healing and Forgiveness	Mark 1:40–45; 2:1–12	Mark 1:1–3:35
2	Responding to God's Word / Faith Through Trials	Mark 4:1–20, 35–41	Mark 4:1–5:20
3	Step Out in Faith / Testing Faith	Mark 5:21–42; 6:45–51	Mark 5:21–6:56
4	God's Truth Versus Tradition / True Discipleship	Mark 7:1–23; 8:34–38	Mark 7:1–8:38
5	Faith to Overcome / Salvation Through Faith	Mark 9:14–29; 10:17–31	Mark 9:1–10:52
6	The Greatest Commandment / Adoration	Mark 12:28–34; 14:3–9	Mark 11:1–16:20

Generally, the ideal size you will want for the group is between eight to ten people, which ensures everyone will have enough time to participate in discussions. If you have more people, you might want to break up the main group into smaller subgroups. Encourage those who show up at the first meeting to commit to attending the duration of the study, as this will help the group members get to know each other, create stability for the group, and help you know how to prepare each week.

Each of the lessons begins with a brief reflection that highlights the theme you will be discussing that week. As you begin your group time, have the group members briefly respond to the opening question to get them thinking about the topic at hand. Some people may want to tell a long story in response to one of these questions, but the goal is to keep the answers brief. Ideally, you want everyone in the group to get a chance to answer, so try to keep the responses to just a few minutes. If you have more talkative group members, say up front that everyone needs to limit his or her answer to two minutes.

Give the group members a chance to answer, but tell them to feel free to pass if they wish. With the rest of the study, it's generally not a good idea to have everyone answer every question—a free-flowing discussion is more desirable. But with the opening reflection question, you can go around the circle. Encourage shy people to share, but don't force them.

Before your first meeting, let the group members know how the lessons are broken down. During your group discussion time the members will be drawing on the answers they wrote to the Exploration and Reaction sections, so encourage them to always complete these ahead of time. Also, invite them to bring any questions and insights they uncovered while reading to your next meeting, especially if they had a breakthrough moment or if they didn't understand something they read.

WEEKLY PREPARATION

As the leader, there are a few things you should do to prepare for each meeting:

- *Read through the lesson.* This will help you to become familiar with the content and know how to structure the discussion times.
- *Decide which questions you want to discuss.* Depending on how you structure your group time, you may not be able to cover every question. So select the questions ahead of time that you absolutely want the group to explore.
- *Be familiar with the questions you want to discuss.* When the group meets you'll be watching the clock, so you want to make sure you are familiar with the Bible study questions you have selected. You can then spend time in the passage again when the group meets. In this way, you'll ensure you have the passage more deeply in your mind than your group members.
- *Pray for your group.* Pray for your group members throughout the week and ask God to lead them as they study his Word.
- *Bring extra supplies to your meeting.* The members should bring their own pens for writing notes, but it's a good idea to have extras available for those who forget. You may also want to bring paper and additional Bibles.

Note that in many cases there will not be one "right" answer to the question. Answers will vary, especially when the group members are being asked to share their personal experiences.

STRUCTURING THE DISCUSSION TIME

You will need to determine with your group how long you want to meet each week so you can plan your time accordingly. Generally, most groups like to meet for either sixty minutes or ninety minutes, so you could use one of the following schedules:

Section	60 Minutes	90 Minutes
WELCOME (members arrive and get settled)	5 minutes	10 minutes
REFLECTION (discuss the opening question for the lesson)	10 minutes	15 minutes
DISCUSSION (discuss the Bible study questions in the Exploration and Reaction sections)	35 minutes	50 minutes
PRAYER/CLOSING (pray together as a group and dismiss)	10 minutes	15 minutes

As the group leader, it is up to you to keep track of the time and keep things moving along according to your schedule. You might want to set a timer for each segment so both you and the group members know when your time is up. (Note that there are some good phone apps for timers that play a gentle chime or other pleasant sound instead of a disruptive noise.) Don't feel pressured to cover every question you have selected if the group has a good discussion going. Again, it's not necessary to go around the circle and make everyone share.

Don't be concerned if the group members are silent or slow to share. People are often quiet when they are pulling together their ideas, and this might be a new experience for them. Just ask a question and let it hang in the air until someone shares. You can then say, "Thank you. What about others? What came to you when you reflected on the passage?"

GROUP DYNAMICS

Leading a group through *Life Lessons from Mark* will prove to be highly rewarding both to you and your group members—but that doesn't mean you will not encounter any challenges along the way! Discussions can get off track. Group members may not be sensitive to the needs and ideas of others. Some might worry they will be expected to talk about matters that make them feel awkward. Others may express comments that result in disagreements. To help ease this strain on you and the group, consider the following ground rules:

- When someone raises a question or comment that is off the main topic, suggest you deal with it another time, or, if you feel led to go in that direction, let the group know you will be spending some time discussing it.
- If someone asks a question you don't know how to answer, admit it and move on. At your discretion, feel free to invite group members to comment on questions that call for personal experience.
- If you find one or two people are dominating the discussion time, direct a few questions to others in the group. Outside the main group time, ask the more dominating members to help you draw out the quieter ones. Work to make them a part of the solution instead of the problem.
- When a disagreement occurs, encourage the group members to process the matter in love. Encourage those on opposite sides to restate what they heard the other side say about the matter, and then invite each side to evaluate if that perception is accurate. Lead the group in examining other Scriptures related to the topic and look for common ground.

When any of these issues arise, encourage your group members to follow the words from the Bible: "Love one another" (John 13:34), "If it is possible, as far as it depends on you, live at peace with everyone" (Romans 12:18), and, "Be quick to listen, slow to speak and slow to become angry" (James 1:19).

Thank you again for taking the time to lead your group. May God reward your efforts and dedication and make your time together in this study fruitful for his kingdom.

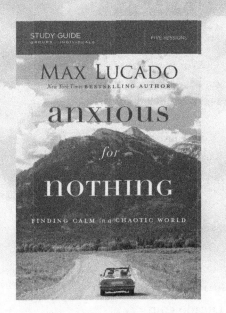
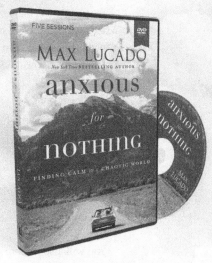

Inspired by what you just read?
Connect with Max.

Listen to Max's teaching ministry, UpWords, on the radio and online. Visit www.MaxLucado.com to get FREE resources for spiritual growth and encouragement, including:

- Archives of UpWords, Max's daily radio program, and a list of radio stations where it airs

- Devotionals and e-mails from Max

- First look at book excerpts

- Downloads of audio, video, and printed material

- Mobile content

You will also find an online store and special offers.

www.MaxLucado.com

1-800-822-9673

UpWords Ministries
P.O. Box 692170
San Antonio, TX 78269-2170

Join the Max Lucado community:

Follow Max on Twitter @MaxLucado
or at Facebook.com/MaxLucado